THE COMPLETE
SLOW COOKER
COOKBOOK FOR UK
2023

Simple and Delicious Slow Cooker Recipes for Busy
Weeknight Meals in the UK

CHARLES GARNER

TABLE OF CONTENT

INTRODUCTION

A slow cooker, is a kitchen appliance that allows you to cook food at a low temperature for a long period of time. It is a convenient and easy way to make delicious and nutritious meals, without the need to spend hours in the kitchen. Slow cookers come in a variety of sizes and styles, making them suitable for any kitchen and lifestyle.

One of the biggest benefits of using a slow cooker is the convenience it offers. Simply add all of the ingredients to the pot in the morning, set the temperature and timer, and come home to a hot and ready meal. This makes it perfect for busy families, working professionals, and anyone looking for a quick and easy way to make dinner.

Slow cookers are energy efficient, as they use less energy than an oven or stovetop. This makes them a great option for those looking to save money on their energy bill. Slow cookers are also easy to clean, with many models featuring non-stick surfaces and dishwasher safe parts.

This UK Slow Cooker Cookbook is a comprehensive guide to creating delicious and nutritious meals using the convenience of a slow cooker. With over 100 recipes, this cookbook offers a wide variety of dishes that are perfect for busy families, those on a budget, and anyone looking to create delicious meals with minimal effort. Many of the recipes in this cookbook use pantry staples and frozen vegetables, making them an easy and affordable option. From hearty stews and soups, to tender meats and flavorful vegetables.

Now, let's go with slow cooking in your life!

CHAPTER 1 THE SLOW COOKER BASICS

WHAT IS A SLOW COOKER?

As the name suggests, a slow cooker is a kitchen appliance that cooks meals low and slow over a long period of time. For example, cooking stew on a stove takes one to two hours, on average. However, with a slow cooker, you can cook the stew for up to approximately 10 hours.

The slow cooker is cheap to buy, easy and economical to use, and above all, it's incredible for getting the best out of budget ingredients. What's makes slow cookers unique, however, is its handoff cooking. It takes a lot of things that happen in the kitchen off your plate, allowing you to get on with other business of living.

A slow cooker can be manual or programmable. The manual slow cooker models offer three temperature settings low, medium, and high. However, they lack a timer and you have to monitor your meals as they cook manually, and turn off the appliance once the food is ready. Some manual slow cookers come with a keep-warm setting, which comes in handy when you need to warm your food.

On the other hand, programmable slow cookers are advanced models that feature digital controls and a timer. This model lets you set the required cooking time, say 6 hours. The timer shows the remaining cooking time on a digital screen. One the time elapses, the slow cooker automatically switches to the keep-warm settings.

FEATURES OF A SLOW COOKER

The slow cooker has three main features:

* The pot:

The pot is the inside part where you toss your ingredients to cook. Many slow cookers come with an oval ceramic pot. The oval shape makes it easy to accommodate ingredients like large cuts meat or roasts.

* Lids:

Generally, slow cookers have a clear plastic or glass lid. The nature of the lid lets you cook and monitor your meals without having to remove it. In some special brands, the slow cooker features a hinged lid, while other hand lids that lock themselves. Having a lid that locks makes it easy to transport food in the slow cooker without spilling

* Temperature settings:

As mentioned above, slow cookers have three temperature settings, namely Low, high, and medium.

Temperature probe: This is an additional feature that pops up on some brands. Generally, the probes come in handy when you want to check the internal temperature, for example, when cooking a large cut of meat.

BENEFITS OF SLOW COOKERS

What you ought to know is that a slow cooker isn't suited to all cooking tasks. However, this modern cooking appliance provides multiple benefits. If you are getting started with slow cookers here are some advantages you'll get:

1. Slow cooking allows the optimal distribution of the flavors in many recipes. In other words, the slow cooker brings out the flavors in your meals.
2. Unlike the standard electric oven, a slow cooker is energy efficient.
3. Besides, this appliance usually supports one-step preparation. It saves preparation time since all you need to is toss all your ingredients, switch on the slow cooker, and let the meal cook, unattended.
4. Moreover, since slow cookers cook food for a long time, they are good at tenderizing less expensive cuts of meat.
5. Most importantly, it's easy to carry your slow cooker. As such, if you have a party away from home, you can pack the appliance and carry it to your destination.

TIPS FOR USING A SLOW COOKER

Many people are skeptical about leaving a slow cooker to cook unattended, hence hesitant to buy a slow cooker. If this sounds familiar, the security concern needs not to be a stumbling block. Instead, you should purchase the appliance and use it for cooking when you are at home. Besides, you should apply the following success tips to get the best out of your appliance:

1. For complete cooking, never cook frozen meat or poultry in the slow cooker. Instead, thaw frozen ingredients in the refrigerator, before tossing them in the slow cooker.
2. Also, never fill your slow cooker less than half or more than two-thirds. Ignoring these limits can adversely affect safety, cooking time, and quality.
3. Whenever it's possible, cook on high temperatures for the first hour, and then switch the slow cooker's settings to low.
4. Most importantly, always ensure the lid is tightly locked during cooking. Remember, every time you remove the lid, you lose about 15 to 20 minutes of cooking time.
5. To prevent curdling, add cream, cheese, and milk during the final hour of cooking.
6. On the other hand, to preserve nutrients soft vegetables, it's advisable you add them during the final 45 minutes of cooking.

CHAPTER 2: BREAKFAST

SAUSAGE HASH BROWN BREAKFAST BAKE

Prep time: 15 minutes | Cook time: 3 hours | Serves 6 to 8

INGREDIENTS:

* 30 g unsalted butter
* 30 g plain flour
* 175 ml low-sodium chicken broth
* 115 ml milk
* Coarse salt and freshly ground pepper, to taste
* 450 g sweet Italian sausage, casings removed
* 3 sweet peppers, thinly sliced
* 900 g rooster potatoes, peeled and grated
* 120 g grated cheddar cheese
* 6 scallions, finely chopped
* Fried eggs, for serving
* Chopped fresh chives, for garnish

DIRECTIONS:

1. Melt butter in a saucepan over medium heat. Whisk in flour and cook for about 1 minute. Add broth and milk and bring to a boil, whisking constantly. Remove from heat and season with salt and pepper. Transfer sauce to a bowl.
2. Heat the saucepan over medium-high heat. Add sausage and cook, breaking up meat with a spoon, until browned, about 5 minutes. Add peppers and continue to cook until peppers are soft, about 5 minutes. Season with salt and pepper. Transfer to a slow cooker, spreading into an even layer.
3. Add potatoes, cheese, and scallions to milk mixture and mix well. Transfer to slow cooker and spread into an even layer. Cover and cook on high until hot and bubbly, about 3 hours (or on low for 6 hours). Serve warm, with fried eggs and topped with chives.

WESTERN OMELETTE BAKE

Prep time: 15 minutes | Cook time: 8 to 9 hours | Serves 10

INGREDIENTS:

* 900 g frozen hash brown potatoes
* 450 g cooked ham, cubed
* 1 medium onion, diced
* 180 g shredded Cheddar cheese
* 12 eggs
* 235 ml milk
* 1 tsp. salt
* 1 tsp. pepper

DIRECTIONS:

1. Layer one-third each of frozen potatoes, ham, onion, and cheese in the bottom of the slow cooker. Repeat 2 times.
2. Beat together eggs, milk, salt, and pepper in a bowl.
3. Pour over mixture in a slow cooker. Cover and cook on low for 8 to 9 hours.
4. Serve with orange juice and fresh fruit, if desired.

FISH CONGEE

Prep time: 10 minutes | Cook time: 4½ hours | Serves 6

INGREDIENTS:

* 300 g long-grain white rice
* 1 (2½-cm) piece fresh ginger, peeled and grated
* 3 L boiling water
* 350 g firm white fish fillets, such as flounder or cod, skin removed, thinly sliced
* Coarse salt, to taste
* Sliced scallions, for serving

DIRECTIONS:

1. Place the rice and ginger into the slow cooker. Add the boiling water and stir. Cover and cook on low until congee reaches consistency of loose porridge, about 4 hours (or on high for 2 hours).
2. Add fish and cook on low until fish falls apart, about 20 minutes more (or on high for 10 minutes). Season to taste with salt and serve with the sliced scallions.

BASIC PORRIDGE

Prep time: 5 minutes | Cook time: 6 hours | Serves 4

INGREDIENTS:

* 10o g dry old-fashioned rolled oats
* 600 ml water
* Dash of salt

DIRECTIONS:

1. Mix together oats, water, and salt in a slow cooker. Cook on low for 6 hours.
2. Stir and serve.

SWEET POTATO AND CORN SCRAMBLE

Prep time: 10 minutes | Cook time: 8 hours | Serves 2

INGREDIENTS:

* 5 g butter, at room temperature, or extra-virgin olive oil
* 4 eggs
* 120 ml semi-skimmed milk
* ⅛ tsp. sea salt
* ½ tsp. smoked paprika
* ½ tsp. ground cumin
* Freshly ground black pepper, to taste
* 150 g finely diced sweet potato
* 175 g frozen corn kernels, thawed
* 75 g diced roasted red peppers
* 2 tbsps. minced onion

DIRECTIONS:

1. Grease the inside of the slow cooker with the butter.
2. In a small bowl, whisk together the eggs, milk, salt, paprika, and cumin. Season with the freshly ground black pepper.
3. Put the sweet potato, corn, red peppers, and onion into the slow cooker. Pour in the egg mixture and stir gently.
4. Cover and cook on low for 8 hours or overnight. Serve warm.

EASY BOSTON BROWN BREAD

Prep time: 5 minutes | Cook time: 3 to 4 hours | Serves 6 to 8

INGREDIENTS:

* 80 g rye flour
* 90 g fine wholemeal flour
* 135 g fine white cornmeal
* 1¾ tsps. bread soda
* ½ tsp. baking powder
* 1 tsp. salt
* 400 ml buttermilk
* 160 g black treacle
* 45 g butter, melted
* 120 g raisins
* 475 ml boiling water
* Rapeseed oil spray

DIRECTIONS:

1. Fold four 30 by 20-cm pieces of aluminium foil in half twice to yield rectangles that measure 15 by 10-cm and grease one side with rapeseed oil spray. Coat inside of four 425-g tins with oil spray.
2. Whisk rye flour, fine wholemeal flour, cornmeal, bread soda, baking powder, and salt together in a large bowl. Whisk buttermilk, black treacle, and melted butter together in a second bowl. Stir raisins into buttermilk mixture. Add buttermilk mixture to flour mixture and stir until combined and no dry flour remains. Divide batter evenly among prepared tins and smooth top with back of greased spoon. Wrap tops of tins tightly with prepared foil, greased side facing batter.
3. Line bottom of a slow cooker with greaseproof paper. Fill the slow cooker with 1¼-cm boiling water (about 475 ml water) and set tins in the slow cooker. Cover and cook until skewer inserted in the centre of loaves comes out clean, 3 to 4 hours on high.
4. Using tongs and sturdy spatula, transfer tins to a wire rack and let cool, uncovered, for 20 minutes. Invert tins and slide loaves onto the rack and let cool completely, about 1 hour. Slice and serve. (Bread can be wrapped tightly in cling film and stored at room temperature for up to 3 days.)

CHEESE AND HAM BREAKFAST SOUFFLÉ

Prep time: 10 minutes | Cook time: 3 to 4 hours | Serves 6

INGREDIENTS:

* 8 slices bread (crusts removed), cubed or torn into squares
* 240 g shredded Cheddar, Swiss, or American cheese
* 150 g cooked, chopped ham
* 4 eggs
* 235 ml light cream or milk
* 235 ml evaporated milk
* ¼ tsp. salt
* 1 tbsp. parsley
* Paprika, to taste
* Rapeseed oil spray

DIRECTIONS:

1. Lightly grease a slow cooker with rapeseed oil spray. Alternate layers of bread, cheese and ham.
2. Beat together eggs, milk, salt, and parsley in a bowl.
3. Pour over bread in a slow cooker and sprinkle with paprika.
4. Cover and cook on low for 3 to 4 hours. (The longer cooking time yields a firmer, dryer dish.)
5. Serve warm.

CHAPTER 3: VEGETABLE

BRAISED BUTTERNUT SQUASH WITH PECANS

Prep time: 15 minutes | Cook time: 4 to 5 hours | Serves 4 to 6

INGREDIENTS:

* 235 ml vegetable or chicken broth
* 2 garlic cloves, peeled and smashed
* 2 sprigs fresh thyme
* Salt and pepper, to taste
* 900 g butternut squash, peeled, halved lengthwise, deseeded, and sliced 2-cm thick
* 30 ml extra-virgin olive oil
* 1 tsp. grated lemon zest plus 2 tsps. juice
* 35 g toasted and chopped pecans
* 35 g dried cranberries
* 1 tbsp. minced fresh parsley

DIRECTIONS:

1. Combine broth, garlic, thyme sprigs, and ¼ tsp. salt in a slow cooker. Nestle squash into a slow cooker. Cover and cook until squash is tender, 4 to 5 hours on low or 3 to 4 hours on high.
2. Using a slotted spoon, transfer squash to a serving dish, brushing away any garlic cloves or thyme sprigs that stick to squash. Whisk oil and lemon zest and juice together in the bowl. Season with salt and pepper to taste. Drizzle squash with dressing and sprinkle with pecans, cranberries, and parsley. Serve.

BRAISED PEAS WITH LETTUCE AND ONIONS

Prep time: 20 minutes | Cook time: 2½ to 3½ hours | Serves 8

INGREDIENTS:

* 1 medium-size head Boston lettuce
* 1 sprig fresh thyme, savoury, or mint
* 8 white boiling onions (16 if they are really tiny), peeled
* 120 g unsalted butter, softened
* ½ tsp. sugar
* ½ tsp. salt
* ½ tsp. ground white pepper
* 1.6 to 1.8 kg fresh peas in the pod, or 680 g frozen garden peas (not petites), thawed
* 60 ml water

DIRECTIONS:

1. Coat the slow cooker with rapeseed oil spray or butter; line the bottom and sides with the outer lettuce leaves. Reserve some leaves for the top. Open the lettuce heart, place the single herb sprig inside, and tie with kitchen twine. Put it in the cooker and add the onions.
2. In a small bowl, mash together the butter, sugar, salt, and pepper. Add to the bowl of shelled peas and, with your hands, gently squeeze the butter into the mass of peas to coat them; it is okay if some peas are bruised, but try not to crush any. Pack the peas around the heart of lettuce in the cooker and top with more lettuce leaves. Add the water. Cover and cook on high for 30 minutes to get the pot heated up.
3. Reduce the heat setting to low and cook until the peas are tender, 2 to 3 hours. At 2 hours, lift the cover to check their progress. Remove the lettuce leaves and the lettuce heart, and serve the hot peas from the crock.

GARLIC MUSHROOMS WITH CRÈME FRAÎCHE

Prep time: 15 minutes | Cook time: 2 to 3 hours | Serves 6 to 10

INGREDIENTS:

* 680 g chestnut or white mushrooms, stems trimmed
* 235 ml vegetable broth
* 30 ml dry white or red wine
* 3 cloves garlic, chopped
* ⅓ bunch spring onions (white and a few-cm of green parts), chopped
* 1¼ tsps. dried Italian herbs or herbs de Provence
* 100 g crème fraîche (optional)
* 30 g unsalted butter
* Sea salt and freshly ground black pepper, to taste

DIRECTIONS:

1. Combine the mushrooms, broth, wine, garlic, spring onions, and herbs in the cooker; stir to mix well.
2. Cover and cook on high for 2 to 3 hours, or on low for 4 to 6 hours, until the mushrooms are tender. Check at the halfway point. Stir in the crème fraîche (if using) and butter. Season to taste and serve hot, or set aside to cool and then refrigerate, covered, in the poaching liquid. The mushrooms will keep in the refrigerator for up to 4 days.

SAKE-COOKED ASPARAGUS

Prep time: 10 minutes | Cook time: 1¼ to 1½ hours | Serves 4 to 5

INGREDIENTS:

* 550 to 700 g asparagus
* 15 ml olive oil
* 15 ml sake
* 1 tsp. soy sauce
* Pinch of brown sugar
* Pinch of salt
* 1 to 2 tsps. toasted sesame seeds, for garnish (optional)

DIRECTIONS:

1. Wash and drain the asparagus. One by one, hold each spear in both of your hands. Bend the spear at the stem end until the end snaps off. Discard the stem end. Put the asparagus in the slow cooker. Drizzle in the olive oil, sake, and soy sauce. Sprinkle with the brown sugar and salt. With your hands, gently toss the asparagus to coat them lightly with the seasonings. Cover and cook on high until tender when pierced with a sharp knife, 1¼ to 1½ hours.
2. Use a pair of tongs to place the asparagus on a serving platter. Pour the liquid from the crock over the asparagus. Sprinkle with the toasted sesame seeds just before serving.

SQUASH WITH MAPLE ORANGE GLAZE

Prep time: 15 minutes | Cook time: 3 to 4 hours | Serves 4 to 6

INGREDIENTS:

* 2 tsps. grated orange zest plus 118 ml juice
* 5 whole cloves
* 1 cinnamon stick
* 2 small squashes (455 g each), quartered pole to pole and seeded
* Salt and pepper, to taste
* 60 ml maple syrup
* ⅛ tsp. ground coriander
* Pinch cayenne pepper
* 35 g hazelnuts, toasted, skinned, and chopped
* 1 tbsp. chopped fresh parsley

DIRECTIONS:

1. Combine 235 ml water, orange juice, cloves, and cinnamon stick in a slow cooker. Season squashes with salt and pepper and shingle cut side down in a slow cooker. Cover and cook until squashes are tender, 3 to 4 hours on low or 2 to 3 hours on high.
2. Using tongs, transfer squashes to the serving dish, brushing away any cloves that stick to squashes. Microwave maple syrup, coriander, cayenne, and orange zest in bowl until heated through, about 1 minute. Season with salt and pepper to taste. Drizzle glaze over squashes and sprinkle with hazelnuts and parsley. Serve.

CIDER BUTTERNUT SQUASH PURÉE

Prep time: 15 minutes | Cook time: 5 to 6 hours | Serves 6 to 8

INGREDIENTS:

* 1.4 kg butternut squash, peeled, deseeded, and cut into 2½-cm pieces
* 115 ml apple cider, plus extra as needed
* Salt and pepper, to taste
* 60 g unsalted butter, melted
* 30 ml double cream, warmed
* 20 g brown sugar, plus extra for seasoning

DIRECTIONS:

1. Combine squash, cider, and ½ tsp. salt in a slow cooker. Press 16 by 15-cm sheet of greaseproof paper firmly onto squash, folding down edges as needed. Cover and cook until squash is tender, 5 to 6 hours on low or 3 to 4 hours on high.
2. Discard greaseproof. Mash squash with potato masher until smooth. Stir in melted butter, cream, and sugar. Season with salt, pepper, and extra sugar to taste. Serve. (Squash can be held on warm or low setting for up to 2 hours; adjust consistency with extra hot cider as needed before serving.)

INDIA-SPICED CHICKPEAS AND POTATOES

Prep time: 20 minutes | Cook time: 10 hours | Serves 6

INGREDIENTS:

* 15 ml rapeseed oil
* 2 tsps. cumin seeds
* 2 bay leaves
* 7 cm piece cassia bark
* 2 medium onions, thinly sliced
* 1 tsp. salt
* 1 tbsp. freshly grated ginger
* 6 garlic cloves, finely chopped
* 2 fresh green chilis, chopped
* 300 g dried chickpeas, washed
* 2 red potatoes, peeled and diced
* 2 medium tomatoes, finely chopped
* 1 tsp. Kashmiri chilli powder
* 2 tsps. ground coriander seeds
* ½ tsp. turmeric
* 950 ml hot water
* 15 ml fresh lemon juice
* Roughly chopped fresh coriander leaves, for garnish
* 1 tsp. chaat masala
* 2 fresh green chilis, sliced lengthwise

DIRECTIONS:

1. Heat the oil in a frying pan (or in the slow cooker if you have a sear setting). Add the cumin seeds, bay leaves, and cassia bark, and cook until fragrant, about 1 minute.
2. Stir in the sliced onions and salt, and cook for 5 to 6 minutes. Add the ginger, garlic, and chopped chilis, and stir for 1 to 2 minutes.
3. Pour the mixture into the slow cooker with the chickpeas, potatoes, tomatoes, chilli powder, coriander seeds, turmeric, and hot water.
4. Cover and cook for 10 hours on low, or for 8 hours on high. Leave on warm until ready to serve.
5. Just before serving, sprinkle with the lemon juice, chopped coriander leaves, chaat masala, and sliced green chillies.

SWEET POTATO ROAST WITH CRÈME FRAÎCHE

Prep time: 10 minutes | Cook time: 3 to 3½ hours | Serves 6 to 8

INGREDIENTS:

* 45 g unsalted butter, room temperature
* 1 tsp. onion powder
* 1 tsp. garlic powder
* 1½ tsps. dried sage
* Coarse salt and freshly ground pepper, to taste
* 6 sweet potatoes, scrubbed and pierced with a fork
* 150 g crème fraîche
* 1 tbsp. mixed fresh herbs, such as flat-leaf parsley, tarragon, and chives, plus more for garnish
* Finely grated zest of 1 lemon

DIRECTIONS:

1. Preheat a slow cooker.
2. In a bowl, combine butter, onion powder, garlic powder, sage, 2 tsps. salt, and ½ tsp. pepper. Rub sweet potatoes with butter mixture, dividing evenly. Tightly wrap each sweet potato in greaseproof paper, then aluminium foil; transfer to the slow cooker. Cover and cook on high until tender when pierced with a knife, 3 to 3½ hours (or on low for 6 to 7); larger potatoes will take longer to cook.
3. Combine crème fraîche, mixed herbs, and lemon zest in a small bowl. Season with salt and pepper. Spread herbed crème fraîche on a serving platter, and top with sliced potatoes and more herbs.

GREEK GREEN BEANS WITH TOMATOES

Prep time: 20 minutes | Cook time: 3 hours | Serves 6 to 8

INGREDIENTS:

* Coarse salt and freshly ground black pepper, to taste
* 45 g extra-virgin olive oil
* 1 large onion, finely chopped
* 3 garlic cloves, thinly sliced
* ⅛ tsp. red-pepper flakes
* 1½ tsps. dried oregano
* 3 plum tomatoes, peeled and coarsely chopped
* 680 g fresh mature green beans, trimmed and halved if large
* 235 ml low-sodium chicken broth
* 1 lemon, cut into wedges, for serving

DIRECTIONS:

1. Preheat a slow cooker.
2. Heat oil in a large frying pan over medium. Add onion and garlic, and sauté until onion is soft, about 10 minutes. Add red-pepper flakes, oregano, 1 tsp. salt, ¼ tsp. black pepper, and tomatoes, and sauté until tomatoes begin to break down, about 5 minutes.
3. Place beans and a pinch of salt in the slow cooker. Spoon tomato mixture over beans in a slow cooker. Pour in broth. Cover and cook on low until beans are tender, about 3 hours. Season with salt and black pepper. Serve with lemon wedges on the side.

LEMON AND PARSLEY FINGERLING POTATOES

Prep time: 10 minutes | Cook time: 5 to 6 hours | Serves 6

INGREDIENTS:

*   900 g fingerling potatoes, unpeeled
*   30 ml extra-virgin olive oil
*   2 scallions, white parts minced, green parts thinly sliced
*   3 garlic cloves, minced
*   Salt and pepper, to taste
*   1 tbsp. chopped fresh parsley
*   1 tsp. grated lemon zest plus 1 tbsp. juice

DIRECTIONS:

1. Combine potatoes, 15 ml oil, scallion whites, garlic, 1 tsp. salt, and ¼ tsp. pepper in a slow cooker. Cover and cook until potatoes are tender, 5 to 6 hours on low or 3 to 4 hours on high.
2. Stir in parsley, lemon zest and juice, scallion greens, and remaining 15 ml oil. Season with salt and pepper to taste. Serve. (Potatoes can be held on warm or low setting for up to 2 hours.)

THYME GARLIC TOMATOES

Prep time: 15 minutes | Cook time: 5 to 6 hours | Serves 4 to 6

INGREDIENTS:

*   6 ripe tomatoes, cored and halved crosswise
*   120 ml extra-virgin olive oil
*   6 garlic cloves, peeled and smashed
*   2 tsps. minced fresh thyme or ¾ tsp. dried
*   Salt and pepper, to taste

DIRECTIONS:

1. Combine tomatoes, oil, garlic, thyme, ¾ tsp. salt, and ¼ tsp. pepper in a slow cooker. Cover and cook until tomatoes are tender and slightly shrivelled around edges, 5 to 6 hours on low or 3 to 4 hours on high.
2. Let tomatoes cool in oil for at least 15 minutes or up to 4 hours. Season with salt and pepper to taste. Serve.

BUTTERY LEEKS WITH THYME

Prep time: 10 minutes | Cook time: 1 to 1½ hours | Serves 6 to 8

INGREDIENTS:

*   4 leeks, split lengthwise and rinsed well
*   Coarse salt and freshly ground pepper, to taste
*   4 to 6 thyme sprigs
*   2 dried bay leaves
*   90 g unsalted butter, cut into small pieces
*   585 ml low-sodium chicken broth
*   60 ml extra-virgin olive oil
*   Juice of 1 lemon

DIRECTIONS:

1. Preheat a slow cooker.
2. Arrange leeks in the slow cooker. Season generously with salt and pepper, scatter with thyme and bay leaves, and dot with butter. Pour in broth. Cover and cook on high until leeks are tender and easily pierced with the tip of a knife, 1 to 1½ hours (or on low for 2½ hours). Discard bay leaves. Drizzle leeks with oil and lemon juice before serving.

CHAPTER 4: GRAINS AND RICE

AROMATIC VEGETABLE PULAO

Prep time: 10 minutes | Cook time: 2 hours | Serves 6

INGREDIENTS:

* 275 g basmati rice
* 15 g rapeseed oil
* 2 bay leaves
* 5-cm piece cinnamon or cassia bark
* 1 tbsp. black peppercorns
* 1 tbsp. cumin seeds
* 1 tbsp. coriander seeds
* 4 green cardamom pods
* 2 black cardamom pods
* 3 cloves

* 2 medium onions, chopped
* 1 tsp. salt
* 1 tbsp. freshly grated ginger
* 1 garlic clove, chopped
* 2 fresh green chilis, chopped
* 1 tsp. turmeric
* Handful mint leaves, chopped
* Handful fresh coriander leaves, chopped
* 585 ml hot water
* 350 g frozen mixed vegetables, thawed

DIRECTIONS:

1. Wash the rice in a few changes of water until the water runs clear. Soak the rice in warm water for 10 minutes.
2. Heat the oil in a frying pan (or in the slow cooker if you have a sear setting). Add the bay leaves, cassia bark, peppercorns, cumin, and coriander seeds, green and black cardamom pods, and cloves. Sauté for 2 minutes until the spices become aromatic.
3. Add the chopped onions and cook for about 5 minutes until soft. Stir in the salt with the ginger, garlic, green chilis, turmeric, mint, and coriander leaves. Transfer to the slow cooker. Then add the rice and hot water. Stir through gently.
4. Cover the slow cooker and cook on high for 1½ hours or 3 hours on low. Stir the rice once during the cooking time.
5. Switch the cooker to the warming function, add the mixed vegetables, and stir through gently. Cover and leave to steam for 20 minutes.
6. Remove the lid and leave the rice to stand for about 5 minutes before fluffing it with a fork to serve.

RATATOUILLE QUINOA BAKE

Prep time: 20 minutes | Cook time: 8 hours | Serves 2

INGREDIENTS:

* 1 tsp. extra-virgin olive oil
* 75 g diced aubergine
* 75 g diced courgette
* ½ tsp. sea salt
* 400 g tinned whole plum tomatoes, undrained, hand-crushed

* 1 tsp. minced garlic
* 30 g minced onion
* 200 g quinoa
* 1 tsp. herbs de Provence
* 350 ml low-sodium chicken or vegetable broth

DIRECTIONS:

1. Grease the inside of the slow cooker with the olive oil.
2. Put the aubergine and courgette in a colander in the sink. Season them liberally with the salt and allow it to rest for 10 minutes, or up to 30 minutes if you have the time.
3. Put the tomatoes, garlic, onion, quinoa, herbs de Provence, and broth in the slow cooker.
4. Rinse the aubergine and courgette under cool water and gently press any excess moisture from the salted vegetables before adding to them to the slow cooker. Mix everything thoroughly.
5. Cover and cook on low for 8 hours. Serve warm.

DOUBLE-CORN SPOONBREAD WITH CHEESE

Prep time: 10 minutes | Cook time: 3 to 3½ hours | Serves 4 to 6

INGREDIENTS:

* 700 ml milk
* 90 g medium-grind yellow cornmeal
* 1¼ tsps. salt
* 60 g unsalted butter, cut into pieces
* 300 g fresh yellow or white corn kernels or thawed frozen baby corn
* 1 tsp. hot pepper sauce, such as Tabasco
* 1 tbsp. baking powder
* 6 large eggs
* 120 g thinly shredded Cheddar cheese
* Rapeseed oil spray

DIRECTIONS:

1. Whisk together the milk, cornmeal, and salt in a large saucepan over high heat until the mixture comes to a boil. Reduce the heat to a simmer and cook until thickened, about 1 minute. Stir in the butter until melted, the corn, and hot pepper sauce. Sprinkle with the baking powder and whisk in the eggs until completely smooth. Fold in the cheese.
2. Coat the slow cooker with rapeseed oil spray. Pour in the batter. Cover and cook on high until the spoonbread looks set but is not quite firm, 3 to 3½ hours. Serve immediately, scooped onto plates.

BARLEY RISOTTO PRIMAVERA

Prep time: 20 minutes | Cook time: 8 hours | Serves 2

INGREDIENTS:

* 1 tsp. extra-virgin olive oil
* 25 g minced onion
* 35 g diced carrot
* 75 g diced courgette
* 75 g diced red bell pepper
* 1 tsp. minced garlic
* 400 g tinned whole plum tomatoes, undrained, hand-crushed
* 30 g tomato puree
* 1 tbsp. Italian herbs
* 175 g pearl barley
* 350 g low-sodium chicken or vegetable broth
* ⅛ tsp. sea salt
* 30 g roughly chopped fresh basil, for garnish

DIRECTIONS:

1. Grease the inside of the slow cooker with the olive oil.
2. Put the onion, carrot, courgette, bell pepper, garlic, tomatoes, tomato puree, Italian herbs, barley, broth, and salt in the slow cooker, and mix thoroughly.
3. Cover and cook on low for 8 hours, until the barley is tender and all the liquid is absorbed.
4. Garnish each serving with the fresh basil.

TEX-MEX QUINOA SALAD

Prep time: 10 minutes | Cook time: 8 hours | Serves 2

INGREDIENTS:

* 200 g quinoa, rinsed
* 470 g low-sodium vegetable broth
* 30 g minced onion
* 1 tsp. minced garlic
* 75 g corn kernels
* 75 g black beans, drained and rinsed
* 120 g tinned diced tomatoes, undrained
* ½ jalapeño pepper, deseeded and minced
* 1 tsp. ground cumin
* ½ tsp. smoked paprika
* ⅛ tsp. sea salt

DIRECTIONS:

1. Put all the ingredients into the slow cooker and stir everything to mix thoroughly.
2. Cover and cook on low for 8 hours. Serve warm.

PARMESAN POLENTA

Prep time: 5 minutes | Cook time: 6 hours | Serves 8

* 1.75 L water
* 270 g coarse-ground yellow polenta
* 1½ tsps. salt
* 120 g unsalted butter
* 120 g grated or shredded Parmesan or Italian fontina cheese

INGREDIENTS:

DIRECTIONS:

1. Whisk the water, polenta, and salt together in the slow cooker for a few seconds. Cover and cook on high for 30 minutes to 1 hour to heat the water.
2. Stir with a wooden spoon, cover, turn the cooker to low, and cook for about 5 hours, stirring occasionally. The polenta will thicken quite quickly after 2 hours, sort of expand magically in the cooker, and look done, but it will need the extra time to cook all the grains evenly. At 5 hours, taste and make sure the desired consistency has been reached and all the grains are tender. The longer the polenta cooks, the creamier it will become. When done, it will be smooth, very thick (yet pourable), and a wooden spoon will stand up by itself without falling over (the true test). The polenta will be fine on low for an additional hour, if necessary. Add a bit more hot water if it gets too stiff.
3. To serve as a mound of soft polenta, portion out with an oversized spoon onto plates or into shallow soup bowls. Top each serving with a pat of the butter and sprinkle with some of the cheese. Serve immediately.

SAUSAGE SPANISH BROWN RICE

Prep time: 15 minutes | Cook time: 8 to 9 hours | Serves 6

INGREDIENTS:

* 20 g diced yellow onion
* 1 clove garlic, minced
* 1 medium-size red bell pepper, deseeded, and coarsely chopped
* 450 g tinned crushed tomatoes, with their juice
* 350 ml water
* 2 tsps. chilli powder
* 2 tsps. Worcestershire sauce
* 135 g short-grain brown rice
* 1 tbsp. chopped jalapeño
* 450 g fully cooked spicy sausage, diced

DIRECTIONS:

1. Combine all the ingredients in the slow cooker and stir to evenly distribute.
2. Cover and cook on low for 8 to 9 hours. Serve hot.

PUMPKIN CHEESE GRITS

Prep time: 10 minutes | Cook time: 3 to 3½ hours | Serves 4

INGREDIENTS:

* 120 g coarse, stone-ground grits
* 350 ml water
* 235 ml evaporated milk
* 1 tsp. salt
* 120 g mashed cooked pumpkin
* A few grinds of black pepper
* 120 g unsalted butter
* 60 g finely shredded Cheddar cheese

DIRECTIONS:

1. Combine the grits and some cold water in a bowl (the husks will rise to the top). Drain in a mesh strainer.
2. Combine the grits, 350 ml of water, evaporated milk, and salt in the slow cooker. With a wooden or plastic spoon, stir for 15 seconds. Add the pumpkin and pepper, cover, and cook on high for 3 to 3½ hours or on low for 7 to 9 hours, until thick and creamy.
3. Stir in the butter and cheese, cover, turn off the cooker, and let the mixture rest for 10 minutes to melt the butter and cheese. Serve immediately.

DUCK BREASTS WITH PORT AND ORANGE SAUCE

Prep time: 10 minutes | Cook time: 6 to 7 hours | Serves 4

INGREDIENTS:

* 30 g unsalted butter
* 4 boneless duck breast halves, with skin (700 g total)
* 75 ml port wine
* Grated zest of 1 orange
* 1 tsp. salt
* ⅛ tsp. freshly ground black pepper
* 15 g cornflour
* 60 ml milk

DIRECTIONS:

1. Melt the butter in a large frying pan (not a non-stick one) over medium-high heat. When it foams, add the duck, skin side down, and cook until deep golden brown on both sides, 2 to 3 minutes per side. Add the port and bring to a boil. Being careful of long sleeves and dangling hair, touch a long lit match to the liquid in the pan and turn off the heat. The liquid will catch fire and burn for about 30 seconds, then the flames will die out. With a slotted spoon, transfer the duck to the slow cooker. Return the liquid in the pan to a boil and cook briefly, scraping up any browned bits stuck to the pan. Pour over the duck, then sprinkle with the orange zest, salt, and pepper. Cover and cook on low for 6 to 7 hours.
2. Preheat the oven to 190°C. With a slotted spoon, transfer the duck to a shallow baking dish. Tent with aluminium foil and keep warm in the oven while you finish the sauce.
3. Skim and discard as much fat as possible from the liquid in the cooker, then pour into a small saucepan. In a small bowl, stir the cornflour into the milk to make a smooth slurry. Bring the sauce to a boil, add the slurry, and cook, stirring, until it thickens, 3 to 4 minutes. Taste for salt and pepper. Serve the duck with the sauce.

SPICY CHICKEN AND BEAN CHILLI

Prep time: 15 minutes | Cook time: 8 to 10 hours | Serves 4

INGREDIENTS:

* 45 ml olive oil
* 2 medium onions, finely chopped
* 1 medium red bell pepper, deseeded and finely chopped
* 1 medium green bell pepper, deseeded and finely chopped
* 30 g chipotle chilli paste
* 1 tsp. ground cumin
* 1 tsp. dried oregano
* 2 L chicken broth
* 4 corn tortillas, torn into small pieces
* 800 g tinned small white beans, drained and rinsed
* 400 g cooked chicken or turkey
* 450 g frozen corn, thawed
* 15 g finely chopped fresh coriander
* 250 g finely shredded mild cheddar cheese, for garnish
* 500 g soured cream, for garnish

DIRECTIONS:

1. Heat the oil in a large frying pan over medium-high heat. Add the onions, bell peppers, chiles, cumin, and oregano and sauté until the vegetables are softened, 5 to 7 minutes.
2. Transfer the contents of the frying pan to the insert of a slow cooker. Add the broth, tortillas, beans, chicken, and corn.
3. Cover the slow cooker and cook on low for 8 to 10 hours, until the chilli is thick and the beans and vegetables are tender. Stir in the coriander.
4. Serve each bowl garnished with cheese and soured cream.

HEARTY PAELLA

Prep time: 30 minutes | Cook time: 2 to 3 hours | Serves 6 to 8

INGREDIENTS:

* 1 onion, finely chopped
* 30 ml extra-virgin olive oil
* 6 garlic cloves, minced
* 30 g tomato puree
* 1 tsp. smoked paprika
* ¼ tsp. cayenne pepper
* Pinch saffron threads, crumbled
* Salt and pepper, to taste
* 375 g long-grain white rice, rinsed
* 225 g clam juice

* 155 ml water
* 75 ml dry sherry
* 680 g boneless, skinless chicken thighs, trimmed and halved
* 230 g Spanish-style chorizo sausage, cut into 1¼-cm pieces
* 450 g extra-large shrimp, peeled, deveined, and tails removed
* 75 g frozen peas, thawed
* 80 g roasted red peppers, rinsed, patted dry, and thinly sliced
* 2 tbsps. chopped fresh parsley
* Rapeseed oil spray
* Lemon wedges, for serving

DIRECTIONS:

1. Line slow cooker with aluminium foil collar and lightly coat with rapeseed oil spray.
2. Microwave onion, oil, garlic, tomato puree, paprika, cayenne, saffron, and 1 tsp. of salt in a bowl, stirring occasionally, until onion is softened, about 5 minutes. Transfer to prepared slow cooker. Stir in rice.
3. Microwave clam juice, water, and sherry in the bowl until steaming, about 5 minutes. Transfer to a slow cooker. Season chicken with salt and pepper and arrange in an even layer on top of rice. Scatter chorizo over chicken. Gently press 16 by 15-cm sheet of greaseproof paper onto surface of chorizo, folding down edges as needed. Cover and cook until liquid is absorbed and rice is just tender, 2 to 3 hours on high.
4. Discard greaseproof and foil collar. Season shrimp with salt and pepper and scatter on top of paella. Cover and cook on high until shrimp is opaque throughout, 20 to 30 minutes.
5. Sprinkle peas and red peppers over shrimp, cover, and let sit until heated through, about 5 minutes. Sprinkle with parsley and serve with lemon wedges.

TURKEY TACO SALAD

Prep time: 15 minutes | Cook time: 4 to 6 hours | Serves 6

INGREDIENTS:

Meat Sauce:

* 680 g ground dark turkey meat
* 450 g tomato salsa

Salad:

* 1 medium firm-ripe avocado
* 350 g thick shredded or chopped iceberg or romaine lettuce
* 120 g corn crisps
* 400 g tinned pinto beans, rinsed, drained, and heated in a saucepan or microwave

* 180 g shredded cheddar cheese
* 450 g tomato salsa
* 2 medium-size ripe tomatoes, coarsely chopped
* 245 g cold soured cream, stirred
* 115 g sliced black olives, drained

DIRECTIONS:

1. Coat the slow cooker with rapeseed oil spray. To make the meat sauce, put the ground turkey and salsa in the cooker. Cover and cook on low until cooked thoroughly, 4 to 6 hours. Stir the sauce.
2. To make the salad, slice the avocado and put all the salad components in separate containers. On each individual plate layer some lettuce, a handful of corn crisps, some of the hot meat, a spoonful or two of hot pinto beans, shredded cheese, some salsa, diced tomatoes, soured cream, avocado, and olives.

SLOW-COOKER CHICKEN ENCHILADAS

Prep time: 25 minutes | Cook time: 4⅓ to 5⅓ hours | Serves 4 to 6

INGREDIENTS:

* 1 onion, finely chopped
* 60 ml rapeseed oil, divided
* 3 tbsps. chilli powder
* 3 garlic cloves, minced
* 2 tsps. ground coriander
* 2 tsps. ground cumin
* 425 g tomato passata, divided
* 2 tsps. sugar
* 450 g boneless, skinless chicken thighs, trimmed
* Salt and pepper, to taste
* 230 g mild cheddar cheese, shredded
* 15 g minced fresh coriander
* 20 g jarred jalapeños, chopped
* 15 ml lime juice
* 12 corn tortillas

DIRECTIONS:

1. Microwave onion, 30 ml of oil, chilli powder, garlic, coriander, and cumin in a bowl, stirring occasionally, until onions are softened, about 5 minutes; transfer to a slow cooker. Stir in tomato sauce and sugar. Season chicken with pepper and nestle into a slow cooker. Cover and cook until chicken is tender, 4 to 5 hours on low.
2. Transfer chicken to a cutting board, let cool slightly, then shred into bite-size pieces using 2 forks. Combine chicken, 175 ml of sauce, ¾ of the cheese, coriander, jalapeños, and lime juice in a large bowl. Season with salt and pepper to taste.
3. Preheat the oven to 235°C. Spread 175 ml of sauce over bottom of a baking dish. Brush both sides of tortillas with remaining 30 ml of oil. Stack tortillas, wrap in damp dish towel, and place on a plate. Microwave until warm and pliable, about 1 minute.
4. Working with 1 warm tortilla at a time, spread 65 ml chicken filling across centre of tortilla. Roll tortilla tightly around filling and place seam-side down in the baking dish. Arrange enchiladas in 2 columns across the width of dish.
5. Pour remaining sauce over enchiladas to cover completely and sprinkle with remaining cheese. Cover dish tightly with greased aluminium foil. Bake until enchiladas are heated through and cheese is melted, 15 to 20 minutes. Let cool for 5 minutes before serving.

PARMESAN CHICKEN POT PIE

Prep time: 25 minutes | Cook time: 4 to 5 hours | Serves 6

INGREDIENTS:

* 900 g boneless, skinless chicken thighs, trimmed
* Salt and pepper, to taste
* 60 ml extra-virgin olive oil, divided
* 230 g chestnut mushrooms, trimmed and sliced ½-cm thick
* 4 carrots, peeled, halved lengthwise, and sliced 1-cm thick
* 1 onion, finely chopped
* 70 g plain flour
* 2 tsps. minced fresh thyme or ½ tsp. dried
* 1 tsp. tomato puree
* 585 ml chicken broth, plus extra as needed
* 15 ml soy sauce
* 1 sheet puff pastry, thawed
* 3o g Parmesan cheese, grated
* 145 g frozen peas, thawed
* 60 ml double cream
* 15 g chopped fresh parsley

DIRECTIONS:

1. Pat chicken dry with kitchen towels and season with salt and pepper.
2. Heat 15 ml of oil in a frying pan over medium-high heat until just smoking. Brown half of chicken, about 4 minutes per side. Transfer to a slow cooker. Repeat with 15 ml of oil and remaining chicken. Transfer to a slow cooker.
3. Heat 15 ml of oil the frying pan over medium heat until shimmering. Add mushrooms, carrots, onion, and ½ tsp. of salt and cook until vegetables are softened and lightly browned, 8 to 10 minutes. Stir in flour, thyme, and tomato puree and cook until fragrant, about 1 minute. Slowly stir in 350 ml of broth, scraping up any browned bits and smoothing out any lumps. Transfer to a slow cooker.
4. Stir remaining 235 ml of broth and soy sauce into a slow cooker. Cover and cook until chicken is tender, 4 to 5 hours on low.
5. Preheat the oven to 205°C. Roll puff pastry into 30 by 23-cm rectangle on a lightly floured surface. Using a paring knife, cut pastry in half lengthwise, then into thirds width wise to create 6 pieces. Cut four 2½-cm slits in each piece and arrange upside down on greaseproof paper-lined baking sheet. Brush pieces with remaining 15 ml of oil, sprinkle with Parmesan and ¼ tsp. of pepper, and bake until puffed and lightly browned, 10 to 15 minutes, rotating sheet halfway through baking. Let pastry cool on the sheet.
6. Transfer chicken to a cutting board, let cool slightly, then pull apart into large chunks using 2 forks. Stir chicken, peas, and cream into filling and let sit until heated through, about 5 minutes. Adjust consistency with extra hot broth as needed. Stir in parsley and season with salt and pepper to taste. Top individual portions with pastry before serving.

CHAPTER 6: LAMB, PORK AND BEEF

BEEF RAGOÛT WITH VEGGIES

Prep time: 25 minutes | Cook time: 7 to 8 hours | Serves 4 to 5

INGREDIENTS:

* 30 ml olive oil
* 900 g lean beef stew meat or beef cross rib roast, trimmed of fat, cut into 6-cm chunks, and blotted dry
* 2 medium-size onions, coarsely chopped
* 2 large tomatoes, peeled, deseeded, and chopped, or 400 g tinned diced tomatoes, with their juice
* 235 ml dry red wine
* 75 g baby carrots
* 2 cloves garlic, minced
* 15 g quick-cooking tapioca
* 1 tsp. dried Italian herb seasoning
* ½ tsp. salt
* ¼ tsp. freshly ground black pepper
* 2 medium-size courgette, ends trimmed, cut in half lengthwise and sliced crosswise into ½-cm-thick half-moons
* 230 g fresh mushrooms, thickly sliced

DIRECTIONS:

1. In a large frying pan over medium-high heat, heat 15 ml of the oil until very hot. Add half of the beef and brown on all sides, 3 to 4 minutes total. Transfer to the slow cooker. Add the remaining 15 ml of oil and brown the remaining beef.
2. Add the onions to the frying pan and brown slightly over medium-high heat. Add the tomatoes and wine and bring to a boil, scraping up any browned bits stuck to the pan; pour into the cooker. Add the carrots, garlic, tapioca, and Italian herbs to the cooker. Cover and cook on low for 6 to 7 hours.
3. Add the salt, pepper, courgette, and mushrooms, cover, turn the cooker to high, and cook for about 45 minutes, until the meat, mushrooms, and courgette are tender. Serve in shallow bowls or on rimmed dinner plates.

MEDITERRANEAN BEEF ROAST

Prep time: 30 minutes | Cook time: 8 to 10 hours | Serves 8

INGREDIENTS:

* 900 g potatoes (about 6 medium), peeled and cut into 5-cm pieces
* 5 medium carrots (about 350 g), cut into 2½-cm pieces
* 15 g plain flour
* 1 boneless beef chuck roast (1½ to 1¾ kg)
* 15 ml olive oil
* 8 large fresh mushrooms, quartered
* 2 celery ribs, chopped
* 1 medium onion, thinly sliced
* 35 g sliced Greek olives
* 30 g minced fresh parsley, divided
* 400 g tinned diced tomatoes, undrained
* 1 tbsp. minced fresh oregano or 1 tsp. dried oregano
* 15 ml lemon juice
* 2 tsps. minced fresh rosemary or ½ tsp. dried rosemary, crushed
* 2 garlic cloves, minced
* ¾ tsp. salt
* ¼ tsp. pepper
* ¼ tsp. crushed red pepper flakes (optional)

DIRECTIONS:

1. Place potatoes and carrots in a slow cooker. Sprinkle flour over all surfaces of roast. In a large frying pan, heat oil over medium-high heat. Brown roast on all sides. Place over vegetables.
2. Add mushrooms, celery, onion, olives and half of the parsley to slow cooker. In a small bowl, mix remaining ingredients; pour over top.
3. Cook, covered, on low 8 to 10 hours or until the meat and vegetables are tender. Remove beef. Stir remaining parsley into vegetables. Serve beef with vegetables.

BALSAMIC PORK CHOPS WITH FIGS

Prep time: 10 minutes | Cook time: 3½ to 4 hours | Serves 6

INGREDIENTS:

* 60 ml olive oil
* 1 tsp. salt
* ½ tsp. freshly ground black pepper
* 6 (2½-cm-thick) pork loin chops
* 12 dried figs, cut in half
* 2 medium onions, cut into half rounds
* 2 tsps. finely chopped fresh sage leaves
* 120 ml balsamic vinegar
* 60 ml chicken broth
* 30 g unsalted butter

DIRECTIONS:

1. Heat the oil in a large frying pan over high heat. Sprinkle the salt and pepper evenly over the pork chops and add the pork to the frying pan.
2. Brown the pork on all sides. Transfer to the insert of a slow cooker. Add the figs to the slow-cooker insert. Add the onions and sage to the same frying pan and sauté until the onions are softened, about 5 minutes. Deglaze the frying pan with the vinegar and scrape up any browned bits from the bottom of the pan. Transfer the contents of the frying pan to the slow-cooker insert and pour in the broth.
3. Cover and cook on high for 3½ to 4 hours or on low for 6 to 8 hours. Carefully remove the pork from the pot and cover with aluminium foil. Using an immersion blender, purée the sauce and whisk in the butter.
4. Return the pork to the slow cooker and set on warm to serve.

PORK CHOPS AND BELL PEPPERS

Prep time: 25 minutes | Cook time: 3½ to 4 hours | Serves 6

INGREDIENTS:

* 60 ml olive oil
* 2 medium onions, cut into half rounds
* 2 medium red bell peppers, deseeded and cut into 1¼-cm slices
* 2 medium yellow bell peppers, deseeded and cut into 1¼-cm slices
* 1 tsp. ground cumin
* 1 tsp. sugar
* 1 tsp. salt
* ½ tsp. freshly ground black pepper
* 800 g tinned crushed tomatoes, with their juice
* 1 tsp. ancho chilli powder
* 6 (2½-cm-thick) pork loin chops

DIRECTIONS:

1. Heat 20 ml of the oil in a large frying pan over medium-high heat. Add the onions, bell peppers, cumin, sugar, salt, and pepper and sauté until the onions begin to turn translucent, about 10 minutes. Add the tomatoes and stir to combine. Transfer the mixture to the insert of a slow cooker. Cover the cooker and set on low.
2. Heat the remaining oil in the frying pan over medium-high heat. Sprinkle the chilli powder evenly over the chops and add to the frying pan. Brown the chops on all sides. Transfer the chops to the slow-cooker insert and spoon some of the sauce over the chops.
3. Cover the slow cooker and cook on high for 3½ to 4 hours or on low for 6 to 8 hours, until the pork is tender.
4. Serve the pork chops with the sauce.

MAPLE PORK CHOPS IN BOURBON

Prep time: 10 minutes | Cook time: 3 to 4 hours | Serves 6

INGREDIENTS:

* 30 ml olive oil
* 1½ tsps. salt
* ½ tsp. freshly ground black pepper
* 6 (2½-cm-thick) pork loin chops
* 30 g unsalted butter
* 2 medium onions, finely chopped
* 120 g ketchup
* 120 ml bourbon
* 120 ml pure maple syrup
* 1 tsp. Tabasco sauce
* 1 tsp. dry mustard
* 120 ml beef broth

DIRECTIONS:

1. Heat the oil in a large frying pan over high heat. Sprinkle the salt and pepper evenly over the pork chops and add to the frying pan.
2. Brown the chops on both sides, adding a few at a time, being careful not to crowd the pan, and transfer to the insert of a slow cooker.
3. Melt the butter in the frying pan over medium-high heat. Add the onions and sauté until they begin to soften, about 5 minutes. Add the remaining ingredients and scrape up any browned bits from the bottom of the pan. Transfer the contents of the frying pan to the slow-cooker insert.
4. Cover and cook on high for 3 to 4 hours or on low for 6 to 8 hours. Skim off any fat from the top of the sauce.
5. Serve from the cooker set on warm.

COUNTRY-STYLE SPARERIBS

Prep time: 10 minutes | Cook time: 8 to 10 hours | Serves 6

INGREDIENTS:

* 1½ kg country-style spareribs
* 1½ tsps. salt
* 30 ml extra-virgin olive oil
* 3 medium onions, finely chopped
* ⅛ tsp. red pepper flakes
* 3 cloves garlic, minced
* 1 tsp. dried oregano
* 120 ml red wine, such as Chianti or Barolo
* 800 g tinned crushed tomatoes, with their juice

DIRECTIONS:

1. Sprinkle the ribs with the salt and arrange in the insert of a slow cooker. Heat the oil in a large frying pan over medium-high heat. Add the onions, red pepper flakes, garlic, and oregano and sauté until the onions are softened, about 5 minutes.
2. Add the wine to the frying pan and stir up any browned bits from the bottom of the pan. Transfer the contents of the frying pan to the slow-cooker insert and stir in the tomatoes. Cover and cook on low for 8 to 10 hours, until the meat is tender. Skim off any fat from the surface of the sauce.
3. Serve the ribs from the cooker set on warm.

SLOW COOKER PORK VERDE

Prep time: 15 minutes | Cook time: 4½ to 5 hours | Serves 8

INGREDIENTS:

* 3 medium carrots, sliced
* 1 boneless pork shoulder butt roast (1½ to 1¾ kg)
* 400 g tinned black beans, rinsed and drained
* 280 g green enchilada sauce
* 10 g minced fresh coriander
* 1 tbsp. cornflour
* 60 ml cold water
* Hot cooked rice, for serving

DIRECTIONS:

1. Place carrots in a slow cooker. Cut roast in half; place in slow cooker. Add the beans, enchilada sauce and coriander. Cover and cook on low for 4½ to 5 hours or until a meat thermometer reads 70°C. Remove roast to a serving platter; keep warm.
2. Skim fat from cooking juices. Transfer the cooking liquid, carrots and beans to a small saucepan. Bring to a boil. Combine cornflour and water until smooth. Gradually stir into the pan. Bring to a boil; cook and stir for 2 minutes or until thickened. Serve with meat and rice.

HONEY MUSTARD PORK ROAST

Prep time: 20 minutes | Cook time: 6 to 7 hours | Serves 8

INGREDIENTS:

* 1 boneless pork shoulder butt roast (1 to 1½ kg)
* ¾ tsp. salt
* ¼ tsp. pepper
* 15 ml rapeseed oil
* 400 g tinned diced tomatoes, drained
* 1 medium onion, chopped
* 400 g tinned beef broth
* 120 ml dry red wine
* 180 g stone-ground mustard
* 6 garlic cloves, minced
* 40 g honey
* 40 g black treacle
* 1 tsp. dried thyme
* 2 tbsps. cornflour
* 30 ml cold water

DIRECTIONS:

1. Sprinkle roast with salt and pepper; brown in oil in a large frying pan on all sides. Transfer to a slow cooker. Add tomatoes and onion; pour broth and wine around meat. Combine the mustard, garlic, honey, black treacle and thyme; pour over pork. Cover and cook on low for 6 to 7 hours or until meat is tender.
2. Remove roast; cover and let stand for 15 minutes before slicing. Meanwhile, skim fat from cooking juices; transfer juices to a small saucepan. Bring to a boil. Combine cornflour and water until smooth; gradually stir into the pan. Bring to a boil; cook and stir for 2 minutes or until thickened. Slice pork and serve with sauce.

PORK SPARERIBS WITH SAUERKRAUT

Prep time: 30 minutes | Cook time: 6 to 7 hours | Serves 4

INGREDIENTS:

* 450 g fingerling potatoes
* 1 medium onion, chopped
* 1 medium Granny Smith apple, peeled and chopped
* 3 slices thick-sliced streaky bacon strips, cooked and crumbled
* 450 g sauerkraut, undrained
* 900 g pork spareribs

* ½ tsp. salt
* ¼ tsp. pepper
* 15 ml rapeseed oil
* 60 g brown sugar
* ¼ tsp. caraway seeds
* 225 g smoked Polish sausage, cut into 2½-cm slices
* 235 ml beer

DIRECTIONS:

1. In a slow cooker, place the potatoes, onion, apple and bacon. Drain sauerkraut, reserving 75 ml of the liquid; add sauerkraut and reserved liquid to slow cooker.
2. Cut spareribs into serving-size portions; sprinkle with salt and pepper. In a large frying pan, heat oil over medium-high heat; brown ribs in batches. Transfer to slow cooker; sprinkle with brown sugar and caraway seeds.
3. Add sausage; pour in beer. Cover and cook on low for 6 to 7 hours or until ribs are tender.

PORK RIBS WITH PEACH SAUCE

Prep time: 20 minutes | Cook time: 5½ to 6½ hours | Serves 4

INGREDIENTS:

* 900 g boneless country-style pork ribs
* 2 tbsps. taco seasoning
* 120 ml mild salsa
* 60 g peach preserves

* 60 ml barbecue sauce
* 150 g chopped fresh peeled peaches or frozen unsweetened sliced peaches, thawed and chopped

DIRECTIONS:

1. In a large bowl, toss pork ribs with taco seasoning. Cover and refrigerate overnight.
2. Place pork in a slow cooker. In a small bowl, combine the salsa, preserves and barbecue sauce. Pour over ribs. Cover and cook on low for 5 to 6 hours or until meat is tender.
3. Add peaches; cover and cook 30 minutes longer or until peaches are tender.

PORK CHILLI VERDE

Prep time: 10 minutes | Cook time: 5 to 6 hours | Serves 12

INGREDIENTS:

* 1 boneless pork shoulder roast (1¾ to 2¼ kg), cut into 2½-cm pieces
* 850 g tinned green enchilada sauce
* 235 g salsa verde
* 115 g tinned chopped green chillies
* ½ tsp. salt
* Hot cooked rice, for serving
* Soured cream (optional)

DIRECTIONS:

1. In a slow cooker, combine pork, enchilada sauce, salsa verde, green chillies and salt. Cook, covered, on low 5 to 6 hours or until pork is tender. Serve with rice. If desired, top with soured cream.

PORK LOIN WITH CRAN-ORANGE SAUCE

Prep time: 20 minutes | Cook time: 4 hours | Serves 6 to 8

INGREDIENTS:

* 30 ml olive oil
* 1 (1½ to 1¾ kg) pork loin roast, tied
* Salt and freshly ground black pepper, to taste
* 1 large sweet onion, coarsely chopped
* 900 g tinned whole-berry cranberry sauce
* Grated zest of 2 oranges
* Juice of 2 oranges (about 235 ml)
* 2 tsps. dried thyme leaves
* 120 ml beef broth

DIRECTIONS:

1. Spray the insert of a slow cooker with rapeseed oil spray or line it with a slow-cooker liner according to the manufacturer's directions.
2. Heat the oil in a large sauté pan over high heat. Sprinkle the roast with 1½ tsps. salt and 1 tsp. pepper and add to the pan.
3. Sauté the pork on all sides until browned. Transfer the roast to the slow-cooker insert. Add the remaining ingredients and stir to combine. Cover the slow cooker and cook the roast on high for 4 hours or on low for 8 hours.
4. Remove the cover, transfer the roast to a cutting board, and cover loosely with aluminium foil. Let the meat rest for 15 minutes. Skim off any fat from the top of the sauce. Stir the sauce and season with salt and pepper.
5. Slice the roast and nap with some of the sauce. Serve the remaining sauce in a gravy boat on the side.

TERIYAKI PORK TENDERLOIN

Prep time: 5 minutes | Cook time: 3 hours | Serves 6

INGREDIENTS:

* 30 ml rapeseed oil
* 2 cloves garlic, minced
* 1 tsp. grated fresh ginger
* 235 ml soy sauce
* 60 ml rice vinegar
* 15 g light brown sugar
* 2 (450 g) pork tenderloins

DIRECTIONS:

1. Whisk the oil, garlic, ginger, soy sauce, vinegar, and sugar together in a bowl until blended. Remove the silver skin from the outside of the pork with a boning knife and discard.
2. Place the tenderloins in a 1-gallon zipper-top plastic bag or 23-by-33-cm baking dish. Pour the marinade over the tenderloins and seal the bag or cover the dish with cling film.
3. Marinate for at least 4 hours or overnight, turning the meat once or twice during that time. Place the marinade and pork in the insert of a slow cooker. Cover and cook on high for 3 hours.
4. Remove the meat from the sauce, cover loosely with aluminium foil, and allow the meat to rest for about 10 minutes. Skim off any fat from the top of the sauce.
5. Cut the meat diagonally in 1-cm-thick slices. Nap each serving of pork with some of the sauce.

BRAISED PORK LOIN IN CIDER

Prep time: 20 minutes | Cook time: 4 hours | Serves 6 to 8

INGREDIENTS:

* 30 ml olive oil
* 120 g Dijon mustard
* 85 g light brown sugar
* 1 (1 to 1½ kg) pork loin roast, rolled and tied
* 1 large onion, finely sliced
* 2 tsps. dried thyme
* 120 ml sweet apple cider or apple juice
* 235 ml beef stock
* 4 large Gala apples, peeled, cored, and cut into 8 wedges each
* 175 ml double cream
* Salt and freshly ground black pepper, to taste
* 450 g buttered cooked wide egg noodles, for serving

DIRECTIONS:

1. Heat the oil in a large sauté pan over medium-high heat. Make a paste of the mustard and sugar and spread over the roast on all sides. Add the roast to the pan and brown on all sides. Add the onion and thyme to the sauté pan and cook until the onion is softened, 3 to 5 minutes.
2. Transfer the roast, onion, and any bits from the bottom of the pan to the insert of a slow cooker. Add the cider and beef stock. Cover the slow cooker and cook on high for 3 hours. Remove the cover and add the apples and cream. Cover and cook on high for an additional 1 hour.
3. Remove the pork from the slow-cooker insert, cover with aluminium foil, and allow to rest for 15 minutes. Season the sauce with salt and pepper. Remove the strings from the roast, cut into thin slices, and serve the pork on the buttered noodles, napping both with some of the sauce.

TANGY PORK CHOP WITH SWEET POTATO

Prep time: 15 minutes | Cook time: 3 hours | Serves 6 to 8

INGREDIENTS:

* 2 tsps. dried thyme
* 2 tsps. salt
* 1 tsp. freshly ground black pepper
* 8 centre-cut 2½-cm-thick boneless pork loin chops
* 30 ml rapeseed oil
* 120 g unsalted butter
* 1 large sweet onion, such as Vidalia, thinly sliced into half rounds
* 4 medium sweet potatoes, peeled and cut into 1¼-cm slices
* 235 ml orange juice

DIRECTIONS:

1. Combine the thyme, salt, and pepper in a small bowl. Sprinkle half the mixture over both sides of the pork chops. Heat the oil in a large frying pan over medium-high heat.
2. Add the pork chops and brown on both sides. Transfer the pork to the insert of a slow cooker. Melt the butter in the same frying pan over medium-high heat. Add the remaining thyme mixture and sauté for 1 minute.
3. Add the onion and sauté until the onion is beginning to soften, about 3 minutes. Transfer the onion to the slow-cooker insert, leaving some of the butter in the frying pan. Cover the onion with the sweet potato slices and pour the orange juice over all.
4. Drizzle the potatoes with the butter remaining in the frying pan. Cover the slow cooker and cook on high for 3 hours or on low for 6 hours, until the sweet potatoes and pork chops are tender.
5. Serve the pork chops with the sweet potatoes and some of the sauce.

ASIAN BBQ BABY BACK RIBS

Prep time: 10 minutes | Cook time: 7½ to 8½ hours | Serves 6

INGREDIENTS:

* 120 ml soy sauce
* 60 ml hoisin sauce
* 2 tsps. grated fresh ginger
* 2 cloves garlic, minced
* 45 g brown sugar
* 1 tbsp. toasted sesame oil
* 120 ml chicken broth
* 4 spring onions, finely chopped, using the white and tender green parts
* 1¾ kg baby back ribs (about 3 slabs), cut to fit the slow cooker

DIRECTIONS:

1. Stir the soy sauce, hoisin, ginger, garlic, sugar, sesame oil, broth, and spring onions together in the insert of a slow cooker. Add the ribs and push them down into the sauce.
2. Cover and cook on low for 7 to 8 hours, until the meat is tender. Remove cover and cook for an additional 30 to 35 minutes.
3. Serve the ribs with the remaining sauce on the side.

SWEET AND SPICED PORK LOIN

Prep time: 25 minutes | Cook time: 4 to 5 hours | Serves 6 to 8

INGREDIENTS:

* 2 medium sweet potatoes, peeled and cut into 2½-cm chunks or wedges
* 2 medium waxy potatoes, peeled and cut into 2½-cm chunks or wedges
* 2 medium red onions, cut into quarters
* 120 ml olive oil
* 1 tsp. ground cumin
* 1½ tsps. fennel seeds
* ½ tsp. ground cinnamon
* ½ tsp. ground ginger
* 45 g brown sugar
* 2 tsps. salt
* 1 tsp. freshly ground black pepper
* 1 (1¾ kg) pork loin roast, rolled and tied
* 120 ml chicken broth

DIRECTIONS:

1. Arrange the vegetables in the insert of a slow cooker. Drizzle 60 ml of the oil over the vegetables and toss to coat. Combine the cumin, fennel seeds, cinnamon, ginger, sugar, salt, and pepper in a small bowl. Sprinkle 1 tbsp. of the rub over the vegetables and toss again.
2. Pat the rest of the rub over the meat, place the meat on the vegetables, and drizzle with the remaining olive oil. Pour in the chicken broth. Cover and cook on high for 4 to 5 hours or on low for 8 to 10 hours, until the pork and vegetables are tender. The roast should register 80°C on an instant-read thermometer.
3. Transfer the pork to a cutting board, cover with aluminium foil, and let rest for 20 minutes. Cut the meat into 1-cm-thick slices and arrange on the centre of a platter. Spoon the vegetables around the meat and serve.

PORK CHOPS WITH PLUM SAUCE

Prep time: 10 minutes | Cook time: 3½ to 4 hours | Serves 6

INGREDIENTS:

*   60 ml olive oil
*   1 tsp. salt
*   ½ tsp. freshly ground black pepper
*   6 (2½-cm-thick) pork loin chops
*   2 medium onions, finely chopped
*   240 g plum preserves
*   30 g Dijon mustard
*   30 ml fresh lemon juice
*   Grated zest of 1 lemon
*   120 g ketchup

DIRECTIONS:

1. Heat the oil in a large frying pan over high heat. Sprinkle the salt and pepper evenly over the pork chops and add to the frying pan. Brown the pork on all sides.
2. Transfer to the insert of a slow cooker. lower heat to medium-high. Add the onions to the frying pan and sauté until the onions are softened, about 3 to 5 minutes. Add the preserves to the frying pan and scrape up any browned bits from the bottom of the pan. Transfer the contents of the frying pan to the slow-cooker insert.
3. Add the mustard, lemon juice and zest, and ketchup and stir to combine. Cover and cook on high for 3½ to 4 hours or on low for 6 to 8 hours. Skim off any fat from the surface of the sauce.
4. Serve the pork chops from the slow cooker set on warm.

PORK TENDERLOIN WITH MANGO SAUCE

Prep time: 20 minutes | Cook time: 3 hours | Serves 6

INGREDIENTS:

*   60 g unsalted butter, melted
*   2 large mangoes, peeled, pitted, and coarsely chopped
*   2 navel oranges, peeled and sectioned
*   30 ml soy sauce
*   120 ml dark rum
*   120 ml beef broth
*   2 (450 g) pork tenderloins
*   2 tbsps. Jamaican jerk seasoning
*   6 spring onions, finely chopped, using the white and tender green parts for garnish

DIRECTIONS:

1. Stir the butter, mangoes, oranges, soy sauce, rum, and broth together in the insert of a slow cooker. Remove the silver skin from the outside of the pork with a boning knife and discard.
2. Rub the jerk seasoning on the pork and arrange it in the slow cooker. Cover and cook on high for 3 hours, until the pork is tender and cooked through.(The pork should register 80ºC on an instant-read thermometer.)
3. Remove the pork from the sauce, cover with aluminium foil, and allow to rest for 20 minutes. Skim off any fat from the top of the sauce.
4. Slice the meat and garnish with the spring onions. Serve the sauce on the side.

CHAPTER 7: FISH AND SEAFOOD

CHEDDAR SALMON SOUFFLÉ

Prep time: 5 minutes | Cook time: 2 to 3 hours | Serves 4

INGREDIENTS:

* 400 g tinned salmon, drained and flaked
* 2 eggs, beaten well
* 75 g seasoned croutons
* 120 g shredded Cheddar cheese
* 2 chicken stock cubes
* 235 ml boiling water
* ¼ tsp. dry mustard (optional)

DIRECTIONS:

1. Grease the interior of your cooker with rapeseed oil spray.
2. Combine salmon, eggs, croutons, and cheese in the slow cooker.
3. Dissolve stock cubes in boiling water in a small bowl. Add mustard, if you wish, and stir. Pour over salmon mixture and stir together lightly.
4. Cover and cook on high 2 to 3 hours, or until mixture appears to be set. Allow to stand 15 minutes before serving.

BUTTERY HALIBUT WITH GARLIC

Prep time: 10 minutes | Cook time: 4¾ hours | Serves 6

INGREDIENTS:

* 240 g unsalted butter
* 120 ml olive oil
* 6 cloves garlic, sliced
* 1 tsp. sweet paprika
* 120 ml lemon juice
* Grated zest of 1 lemon
* 10 g finely chopped fresh chives
* 1 to 1½ kg halibut fillets
* 15 g finely chopped fresh Italian parsley

DIRECTIONS:

1. Combine the butter, oil, garlic, paprika, lemon juice, zest, and chives in the insert of a slow cooker and stir to combine. Cover and cook on low for 4 hours.
2. Add the halibut to the pot, spooning the sauce over the halibut. Cover and cook for an additional 40 minutes, until the halibut is cooked through and opaque.
3. Sprinkle the parsley evenly over the fish and serve immediately.

GREEN CHILLI AND SHRIMP TACOS

Prep time: 25 minutes | Cook time: 6 to 7 hours | Serves 4 to 6

INGREDIENTS:

* 4 poblano chilis, stemmed, deseeded, and cut into 1-cm-wide strips
* 3 onions, halved and thinly sliced
* 45 ml extra-virgin olive oil
* 4 garlic cloves, thinly sliced
* ½ tsp. dried oregano
* Salt and pepper, to taste
* 700 g extra-large shrimp, peeled, deveined, tails removed, and cut into 2½-cm pieces
* 2 tbsps. minced fresh coriander
* 1 tsp. grated lime zest plus 1 tsp. juice
* 12 to 18 corn tortillas, warmed

DIRECTIONS:

1. Toss poblanos and onions with 60 ml oil, garlic, oregano, ½ tsp. salt, and ½ tsp. pepper in slow cooker. Cover and cook until vegetables are tender, 6 to 7 hours on low or 4 to 5 hours on high.
2. Season shrimp with salt and pepper and stir into a slow cooker. Cover and cook on high until shrimp pieces are opaque throughout, 30 to 40 minutes. Strain shrimp mixture, discarding cooking liquid, and return to now-empty slow cooker. Stir in coriander, lime zest and juice, and remaining 15 ml oil. Season with salt and pepper to taste. Serve with tortillas.

CREAMY BRAISED SCALLOPS WITH LEEKS

Prep time: 20 minutes | Cook time: 3 to 4 hours | Serves 4

INGREDIENTS:

* 450 g leeks, white and light green parts only, halved lengthwise, thinly sliced, and washed thoroughly
* 4 garlic cloves, minced
* 1 tsp. extra-virgin olive oil
* 80 ml double cream
* 60 ml dry white wine
* 700 g large sea scallops, tendons removed
* Salt and pepper, to taste
* 30 g grated Pecorino Romano cheese
* 2 tbsps. minced fresh parsley

DIRECTIONS:

1. Microwave leeks, garlic, and oil in bowl, stirring occasionally, until leeks are softened, about 5 minutes; transfer to a slow cooker. Stir in cream and wine. Cover and cook until leeks are tender but not mushy, 3 to 4 hours on low or 2 to 3 hours on high.
2. Season scallops with salt and pepper and nestle into a slow cooker. Spoon portion of sauce over scallops. Cover and cook on high until sides of scallops are firm and centres are opaque, 30 to 40 minutes.
3. Transfer scallops to serving dish. Stir Pecorino into sauce and season with salt and pepper to taste. Spoon sauce over scallops and sprinkle with parsley. Serve.

MISO-GLAZED SESAME BLACK COD

Prep time: 10 minutes | Cook time: 5 hours | Serves 6

INGREDIENTS:

* 120 g white miso paste
* 60 ml rice wine (mirin)
* 45 g light brown sugar
* 5 ml rice vinegar
* 350 ml water
* 900 g black cod (if unavailable, use fresh cod, halibut, sea bass, or salmon)
* 6 spring onions, finely chopped, using the white and tender green parts
* 60 g toasted sesame seeds, for garnish

DIRECTIONS:

1. Combine the miso, rice wine, sugar, rice vinegar, and water in the insert of a slow cooker.
2. Cover and cook on low for 4 hours. Add the cod, spooning the sauce over the top. Cover and cook for an additional 30 to 45 minutes.
3. Remove the cod from the slow-cooker insert and cover with aluminium foil to keep warm. Pour the sauce in a saucepan. Bring to a boil and reduce by half until it begins to look syrupy, about 15 to 20 minutes. Add the spring onions to the sauce.
4. Serve each piece of cod in a pool of the sauce and sprinkle each serving with sesame seeds. Serve any additional sauce on the side.

HERBED PERCH WITH POTATO

Prep time: 10 minutes | Cook time: 1 to 2 hours | Serves 4

INGREDIENTS:

* 300 g tinned cream of celery soup
* 120 ml water
* 450 g perch fillet, fresh or thawed
* 280 g cooked, diced potatoes, drained
* 30 g grated Parmesan cheese
* 1 tbsp. chopped parsley
* ½ tsp. salt
* ½ tsp. dried basil
* ¼ tsp. dried oregano

DIRECTIONS:

1. Combine soup and water. Pour half in the slow cooker. Spread fillet on top. Place potatoes on fillet. Pour remaining soup mix over top.
2. Combine cheese and herbs. Sprinkle over ingredients in a slow cooker.
3. Cover. Cook on high 1 to 2 hours, being careful not to overcook fish.

SALMON WITH WHITE RICE SALAD

Prep time: 20 minutes | Cook time: 1 to 2 hours | Serves 4

INGREDIENTS:

* 400 ml boiling water
* 275 g instant white rice
* 75 ml extra-virgin olive oil
* Salt and pepper, to taste
* 4 (175- to 225-g) skin-on salmon fillets, 3 to 4-cm thick
* 60 ml red wine vinegar
* 20 g honey
* 2 tsps. minced fresh oregano
* 2 garlic cloves, minced
* 230 g cherry tomatoes, quartered
* 15 g fresh parsley leaves
* 60 g feta cheese, crumbled
* Lemon wedges, for serving

DIRECTIONS:

1. Lightly coat slow cooker with rapeseed oil spray. Combine boiling water, rice, 15 ml oil, ½ tsp. salt, and ½ tsp. pepper in prepared slow cooker. Gently press 16 by 15-cm sheet of greaseproof paper onto surface of water, folding down edges as needed.
2. Season salmon with salt and pepper and arrange, skin side down, in even layer on top of greaseproof. Cover and cook until salmon is opaque throughout when checked with tip of paring knife and registers 57ºC (for medium), 1 to 2 hours on low.
3. Using 2 metal spatulas, transfer salmon to serving dish; discard greaseproof and remove any white albumin from salmon. Whisk vinegar, honey, oregano, garlic, and remaining oil together in a bowl. Fluff rice with fork, then gently fold in tomatoes, parsley, feta, and 120 ml vinaigrette. Season with salt and pepper to taste. Drizzle remaining vinaigrette over salmon and serve with salad and lemon wedges.

CITRUS SEA BASS WITH PARSLEY

Prep time: 15 minutes | Cook time: 1½ hours | Serves 4

INGREDIENTS:

* 675 g sea bass fillets, rinsed and blotted dry
* Sea salt and white pepper, to taste
* 1 medium-size white onion, chopped
* 10 g minced fresh flat-leaf parsley
* 1 tbsp. grated lemon, lime, or orange zest or a combination
* 45 ml dry white wine or water
* 15 ml olive oil or toasted sesame oil

For Serving:

* Lemon wedges
* Lime wedges
* Cold tartar sauce

DIRECTIONS:

1. Coat the slow cooker with rapeseed oil spray or butter and arrange the fish in the crock. Season lightly with salt and white pepper, then add the onion, parsley, and zest. Drizzle with the wine and oil. Cover and cook on high for 1½ hours.
2. Carefully lift the fish out of the cooker with a plastic spatula or pancake turner. Serve immediately with lemon and lime wedges and tartar sauce.

OLD BAY LEMON SEA BASS

Prep time: 15 minutes | Cook time: 2 hours | Serves 6

INGREDIENTS:

* 240 g unsalted butter, melted
* 120 ml fresh lemon juice
* Grated zest of 1 lemon
* 2 cloves garlic, minced
* 120 ml olive oil
* 2 tbsps. Old Bay seasoning
* 1 to 1½ kg sea bass fillets, cut to fit the slow-cooker insert
* 6 medium waxy potatoes, cut into ½-cm-thick slices

DIRECTIONS:

1. Stir the butter, lemon juice, zest, garlic, and 30 ml of the olive oil together in a small bowl. Combine the remaining oil and the seasoning in a large mixing bowl.
2. Paint the sea bass with some of the butter sauce and set aside. Toss the potatoes in the seasoned oil. Pour half the butter sauce in the insert of a slow cooker.
3. Place half the potatoes in the bottom of the slow cooker. Place the sea bass on top of the potatoes and pour half the remaining butter sauce over the sea bass. Place the remaining potatoes on top of the sea bass and drizzle with the remaining butter sauce.
4. Cover and cook on high for 1½ hours, until the potatoes begin to turn golden and the sea bass is cooked through and opaque in the middle. Remove the cover and cook for an additional 15 to 20 minutes.
5. Serve immediately.

SUPER EASY BRAISED TUNA

Prep time: 5 minutes | Cook time: 3 to 4 hours | Serves 6

INGREDIENTS:

* 1½ kg tuna fillets
* Olive oil to cover (about 700 ml)
* 1 tsp. coarse sea salt

DIRECTIONS:

1. Place the tuna in the insert of a slow cooker and pour the oil over the tuna. The oil should cover the tuna, and depending on the shape of your slow cooker, you may need to add a bit more oil. Add the salt to the slow-cooker insert.
2. Cover and cook on low for 3 to 4 hours, until the tuna is cooked through and is white. Remove the tuna from the oil and cool completely before using.

LEMONY SEA BASS TAGINE

Prep time: 20 minutes | Cook time: 6 to 7½ hours | Serves 6

INGREDIENTS:

* 900 g sea bass fillets
* 120 ml olive oil
* Grated zest of 1 lemon
* 60 ml lemon juice
* 1 tsp. sweet paprika
* 15 g finely chopped fresh coriander
* 2 cloves garlic, chopped
* 1 medium onion, finely chopped
* 1 tsp. ground cumin
* ½ tsp. saffron threads, crushed
* 800 g tinned crushed tomatoes, with their juice
* 6 medium waxy potatoes, quartered
* 1 tsp. salt
* ½ tsp. freshly ground black pepper
* 15 g finely chopped fresh Italian parsley

DIRECTIONS:

1. Place the fish in a zipper-top plastic bag.
2. Whisk 60 ml of the oil, the zest, lemon juice, paprika, and coriander together in a small bowl. Pour the marinade over the fish in the bag. Seal the bag and refrigerate for at least 1 hour or up to 4 hours.
3. Heat the remaining oil in a large frying pan over medium-high heat. Add the garlic, onion, cumin, and saffron and sauté until the onion is softened, 5 to 7 minutes.
4. Add the tomatoes and stir to combine. Place the potatoes in the bottom of the insert of a slow cooker and sprinkle them evenly with the salt and pepper, tossing to coat. Add the tomato mixture to the insert. Cover and cook on low for 5 to 6 hours, until the potatoes are almost tender.
5. Pour the marinade into the insert and stir the potatoes and sauce to combine. Put the fish on top of the potatoes and spoon some of the sauce over the top. Cook for an additional 1 to 1½ hours, until the sea bass is cooked through and is opaque in the centre.
6. Sprinkle the parsley evenly over the top of the sea bass and serve immediately, scooping up some potatoes and sauce with the fish.

SOLE WITH PIZZAIOLA SAUCE

Prep time: 25 minutes | Cook time: 4¾ hours | Serves 6 to 8

INGREDIENTS:

Pizzaiola Sauce:

* 30 ml extra-virgin olive oil
* 1 medium onion, finely chopped
* 2 tsps. dried oregano
* 2 tsps. dried basil
* Pinch red pepper flakes
* 3 cloves garlic, minced
* 800 g tinned crushed plum tomatoes, with their juice
* 1½ tsps. salt
* ½ tsp. freshly ground black pepper
* 120 ml olive oil
* 1 tbsp. Old Bay seasoning
* 900 g sole fillets
* 60 g finely shredded Mozzarella cheese
* 60 g freshly grated Parmigiano-Reggiano cheese
* 15 g finely chopped fresh Italian parsley

DIRECTIONS:

1. Heat the oil in a small saucepan over medium-high heat. Add the onion, oregano, basil, red pepper flakes, and garlic and sauté until the onion is softened, about 3 minutes.
2. Add the tomatoes, salt, and pepper and stir to combine. Transfer to the insert of a slow cooker.
3. Cover and cook on low for 4 hours.
4. Mix together the oil and seasoning in a shallow dish. Dip each fillet in the oil mixture and roll up from the narrow end.
5. Place the rolled fillets in the slow cooker, wedging the pieces to fit. Spoon the sauce over each roll and sprinkle evenly with the cheese. Cover and cook on low for 35 to 45 minutes, until the fish is cooked through and flakes easily with a fork.
6. Sprinkle the parsley over the fish and serve immediately.

CHEESY HALIBUT WITH SALSA

Prep time: 10 minutes | Cook time: 2½ to 2¾ hours | Serves 6

INGREDIENTS:

* 700 g prepared medium-hot salsa
* 30 ml fresh lime juice
* 1 tsp. ground cumin
* 1 to 1½ kg halibut fillets
* 175 g finely shredded mild cheddar cheese

DIRECTIONS:

1. Combine the salsa, lime juice, and cumin in the insert of a slow cooker and stir. Cover the slow cooker and cook on low for 2 hours.
2. Put the halibut in the cooker and spoon some of the sauce over the top of the fish. Sprinkle the cheese evenly over the fish. Cover and cook for an additional 30 to 45 minutes.
3. Remove the halibut from the slow cooker and serve on a bed of the sauce.

RED SNAPPER FEAST

Prep time: 15 minutes | Cook time: 2 to 3 hours | Serves 8

INGREDIENTS:

* 1½ kg red snapper fillets
* 1 tbsp. minced garlic
* 1 large onion, sliced
* 1 green bell pepper, cut into 2½-cm pieces
* 2 unpeeled courgette, sliced
* 400 g tinned low-sodium diced tomatoes
* ½ tsp. dried basil
* ½ tsp. dried oregano
* ¼ tsp. salt
* ¼ tsp. black pepper
* 60 ml dry white wine or white grape juice

DIRECTIONS:

1. Rinse snapper and pat dry. Place in a slow cooker sprayed with non-fat cooking spray.
2. Mix remaining ingredients together and pour over fish.
3. Cover. Cook on high 2 to 3 hours, being careful not to overcook the fish.

AUTHENTIC SHRIMP AND CRAB GUMBO

Prep time: 25 minutes | Cook time: 3 to 4 hours | Serves 10

INGREDIENTS:

* 450 g okra, sliced
* 30 g butter, melted
* 60 g butter, melted
* 35 g flour
* 1 bunch spring onions, sliced
* 35 g chopped celery
* 2 garlic cloves, minced
* 500 g tinned tomatoes and juice
* 1 bay leaf
* 1 tbsp. chopped fresh parsley
* 1 fresh thyme sprig
* 1½ tsps. salt
* ½ to 1 tsp. red pepper
* 0.7 to 1.1 L water, depending upon the consistency you like
* 450 g fresh shrimp, peeled and deveined
* 225 g fresh crab meat

DIRECTIONS:

1. Sauté okra in 30 g butter until okra is lightly browned. Transfer to a slow cooker.
2. Combine remaining butter and flour in the frying pan. Cook over medium heat, stirring constantly until roux is the colour of chocolate, 20 to 25 minutes. Stir in spring onions, celery, and garlic. Cook until vegetables are tender. Add to a slow cooker. Gently stir in remaining ingredients.
3. Cover. Cook on high 3 to 4 hours.
4. Serve over rice.

MISO-HONEY POACHED SALMON

Prep time: 5 minutes | Cook time: 1½ hours | Serves 8

INGREDIENTS:

*   1½ kg salmon fillets
*   45 g white Miso
*   60 g honey
*   60 ml rice wine (mirin) or dry sherry
*   2 tsps. freshly grated ginger

DIRECTIONS:

1. Place the salmon in the insert of a slow cooker.
2. Combine the miso, honey, rice wine, and ginger in a mixing bowl and stir.
3. Pour the sauce over the salmon in the slow cooker. Cover and cook on high for 1½ hours, until the salmon is cooked through and registers 75ºC on an instant-read thermometer inserted in the centre of a thick fillet.
4. Carefully remove the salmon from the slow-cooker insert with a large spatula. Remove the skin from the underside of the salmon (if necessary) and arrange the salmon on a serving platter.
5. Strain the sauce through a fine-mesh sieve into a saucepan. Boil the sauce, reduce it to a syrupy consistency, and serve with the salmon.

SLOW COOKER POACHED SALMON STEAKS

Prep time: 10 minutes | Cook time: 1½ hours | Serves 4

INGREDIENTS:

*   4 (225 g) salmon steaks or fillets, rinsed and blotted dry
*   235 ml chicken broth or water
*   120 ml dry white wine
*   Sea salt, to taste
*   2 black peppercorns
*   1 sprig fresh dill
*   1 thick slice onion
*   3 sprigs fresh flat-leaf parsley

For Serving:

*   Lemon wedges
*   Cold tartar sauce

DIRECTIONS:

1. Coat the slow cooker with rapeseed oil spray and arrange the salmon in it. The steaks can be set tightly side by side; tuck the ends of fillets under themselves to even out the thickness of the fish so it can cook evenly.
2. Heat the broth and wine in a saucepan or the microwave until boiling. Pour around the salmon. Sprinkle the steaks with some salt, then add the peppercorns, dill, onion slice, and parsley to the liquid around the steaks. Cover and cook on high until the salmon is opaque and firm to the touch, about 1½ hours.
3. Carefully lift the salmon out of the cooker with a rubber spatula or pancake turner. Serve immediately while still hot or cool until lukewarm in the poaching liquid and refrigerate until cold. Accompany with lemon wedges and tartar sauce.

HERBED BRAISED FLOUNDER

Prep time: 5 minutes | Cook time: 3 to 4 hours | Serves 6

INGREDIENTS:

* 900 g flounder fillets, fresh or frozen
* ½ tsp. salt
* 175 ml chicken broth
* 30 ml lemon juice
* 2 tbsps. dried chives
* 2 tbsps. dried minced onion
* ½ to 1 tsp. leaf marjoram
* 4 tbsps. chopped fresh parsley

DIRECTIONS:

1. Wipe fish as dry as possible. Cut fish into portions to fit slow cooker.
2. Sprinkle with salt.
3. Combine broth and lemon juice. Stir in remaining ingredients.
4. Place a meat rack in the slow cooker. Lay fish on the rack. Pour liquid mixture over each portion.
5. Cover. Cook on high 3 to 4 hours.

SMOKY SALMON FETTUCCINE

Prep time: 10 minutes | Cook time: 1 to 2 hours | Serves 4

INGREDIENTS:

* 470 ml double cream
* 85 to 115 g top quality lox or smoked salmon, chopped or flaked into 1¼-cm pieces
* 450 g fresh fettuccine, regular egg or spinach flavoured
* 30 ml olive oil (optional)
* Freshly ground black pepper, to taste

DIRECTIONS:

1. Combine the cream and the lox in the slow cooker. Cover and cook on low until very hot, 1 to 2 hours.
2. Meanwhile, cook the fettuccine in boiling water until tender to the bite, about 3 minutes. Take care not to overcook. Toss with the olive oil if the pasta is to stand for over 5 minutes. Add the fettuccine to the hot sauce and toss to coat evenly. If your cooker is large enough, just add the pasta to the cooker; if not, pour the sauce over the pasta in a shallow, heated bowl. Garnish with a few grinds of black pepper and serve immediately.

CHAPTER 8: SOUP AND STEW

HEARTY ITALIAN VEGETABLE SOUP

Prep time: 15 minutes | Cook time: 7½ to 8½ hours | Serves 6

INGREDIENTS:

* 45 ml olive oil
* 1 medium-size yellow onion, chopped
* 2 small carrots, diced
* 2 ribs celery, chopped
* 2 small courgette, ends trimmed and cubed
* 400 g tinned red cannellini beans, rinsed, drained, and half the beans mashed
* 1 tsp. salt
* 1 bay leaf
* Freshly ground black pepper, to taste
* 15 g packed fresh flat-leaf parsley leaves, chopped
* 800 g tinned whole tomatoes, mashed, with their juice
* 285 g frozen broad beans
* 585 ml chicken broth
* 5 leaves Swiss chard, chopped, or ½ small head Chinese cabbage, cored and chopped
* 115 ml dry red wine
* 35 g elbow macaroni or little shells
* Freshly grated Parmesan cheese, for serving

DIRECTIONS:

1. In a large frying pan, heat the olive oil over medium heat. Add the onion, carrots, celery, and courgette and cook, stirring often, until just softened, about 5 minutes. Transfer to the slow cooker and add the cannellini beans, salt, bay leaf, pepper, parsley, tomatoes and their juice, broad beans, and broth. Add water to come about 2½-cm above the vegetables. Cover and cook on low for 5 hours.
2. Add the Swiss chard and wine, cover, and continue to cook on low for another 2 to 3 hours. Remove the bay leaf.
3. Stir in the pasta, cover, and cook on high until the pasta is just tender, about 30 minutes. Ladle into soup bowls and serve hot with lots of Parmesan.

WHITE BEAN AND BACON SOUP

Prep time: 15 minutes | Cook time: 8¼ to 9¼ hours | Serves 4 to 6

INGREDIENTS:

* 360 g dried cannellini or broad beans, picked over, soaked overnight, and drained
* 2 to 3 strips streaky bacon, cooked, drained, and chopped
* 1 small yellow onion, finely chopped
* 1 rib celery, minced
* 1 small carrot, minced
* 1 bouquet garni: ½ tsp. dried oregano, 3 sprigs fresh flat-leaf parsley, ½ fresh sage leaf, and 1 bay leaf, wrapped in cheesecloth and tied with kitchen twine
* 1.4 L chicken broth or water
* Salt, to taste
* ¼ tsp. freshly ground black pepper, or more to taste
* 115 ml double cream (optional)

DIRECTIONS:

1. Combine the beans, bacon, onion, celery, carrot, bouquet garni, and broth in the slow cooker. Cover and cook on low for 8 to 9 hours.
2. Remove the bouquet garni and discard. Purée about one-third of the soup in a food processor or with a handheld immersion blender. Season with salt, then add the pepper and cream, if using, cover, and continue to cook on low 15 minutes longer. Ladle into soup bowls and serve hot.

BEEF BARLEY SOUP WITH VEGGIES

Prep time: 10 minutes | Cook time: 5 to 7 hours | Serves 12

INGREDIENTS:

* 450 g lean stewing meat, cut into bite-sized pieces
* 75 g onions, chopped
* 35 g cut green beans, fresh or frozen
* 70 g corn, fresh or frozen
* 1 L beef broth
* 830 g tinned tomatoes
* 340 g low-sodium tomato or V8 juice
* 100 g pearl barley, uncooked
* 235 ml water

DIRECTIONS:

1. Combine all ingredients in a slow cooker.
2. Cover. Cook on high 5 to 7 hours, until vegetables are cooked to your liking.

ITALIAN BEEF MINESTRONE

Prep time: 15 minutes | Cook time: 6 hours | Serves 12

INGREDIENTS:

* 450 g extra-lean beef mince
* 1 large onion, chopped
* 1 clove garlic, minced
* 800 g tinned tomatoes
* 400 g tinned cannellini beans, drained
* 285 g frozen corn
* 2 ribs celery, sliced
* 2 small courgette, sliced
* 100 g macaroni, uncooked
* 585 ml hot water
* 2 beef stock cubes
* ½ tsp. salt
* 2 tsps. Italian seasoning

DIRECTIONS:

1. Brown beef mince in non-stick frying pan.
2. Combine browned beef mince, onion, garlic, tomatoes, cannellini beans, corn, celery, courgette, and macaroni in a slow cooker.
3. Dissolve stock cubes in hot water. Combine with salt and Italian seasoning. Add to a slow cooker.
4. Cover. Cook on low 6 hours.

GARLIC AND ONION SOUP

Prep time: 10 minutes | Cook time: 6 to 7 hours | Serves 4

INGREDIENTS:

* 4 heads garlic
* 1 large yellow onion, chopped
* 1.2 L chicken broth
* 170 g tomato puree
* 45 ml extra-virgin olive oil
* Hot fresh crusty bread, for serving

DIRECTIONS:

1. Fill a small deep saucepan with water and bring to a boil. Separate the garlic heads into cloves and toss them into the boiling water; blanch for 1 minute exactly. Drain the garlic cloves in a colander and rinse under cold running water; peel with a paring knife.
2. Combine the garlic cloves, onion, broth, and tomato puree in the slow cooker and stir to blend. Cover and cook on low for 6 to 7 hours.
3. Purée the soup with a handheld immersion blender or transfer to a food processor or blender and purée in batches. Before serving, add the olive oil. Ladle into soup bowls and serve hot with fresh crusty bread. You can drizzle the top of the soup with a bit more olive oil if you like.

NUTMEG CARROT SOUP

Prep time: 15 minutes | Cook time: 6 to 8 hours | Serves 8

INGREDIENTS:

* 60 ml olive oil
* 2 medium-size yellow onions, chopped
* 2 large rooster potatoes, peeled and chopped
* 1.4 kg carrots (about 15 medium-size), scrubbed, tops cut off, and chopped
* 1 or 2 small cloves garlic, pressed
* ½ tsp. each dried thyme and marjoram
* 1 to 1½ L water or chicken broth, plus more as needed
* 40 g honey
* ½ to 1 tsp. freshly grated nutmeg, to your taste
* Sea salt and freshly ground black pepper, to taste

DIRECTIONS:

1. Heat the oil in a large frying pan over medium heat. Add the onions and cook until softened, 6 to 8 minutes, stirring often to cook evenly.
2. Put the potatoes, carrots, garlic, and herbs in the slow cooker; add the onions and oil, scraping them out of the pan. Add enough of the water to cover everything. Cover and cook on high for 1 hour.
3. Turn the cooker to low and cook until the vegetables are soft, 5 to 7 hours. Purée in batches in a food processor or right in the slow cooker with a handheld immersion blender; the soup will be nice and thick. Stir in the honey and grate the nutmeg right over the crock. Season with salt and pepper. Keep warm on low without letting it come to a boil until serving. Ladle the hot soup into bowls and enjoy.

LEMONY RED LENTIL SOUP

Prep time: 10 minutes | Cook time: 6 to 7 hours | Serves 6

INGREDIENTS:

* 30 ml olive oil
* 1 medium-size yellow onion, finely chopped
* 2 ribs celery, chopped
* 450 g dried red lentils, picked over and rinsed
* 1 tsp. ground cumin
* 1 tsp. ground turmeric
* ¾ tsp. ground coriander
* 30 ml fresh lemon juice
* 1½ L chicken or vegetable broth
* Salt and freshly ground black pepper, to taste (optional)

DIRECTIONS:

1. In a large frying pan, heat the olive oil over medium heat. Add the onion and celery and cook, stirring often, until just softened, about 5 minutes. Transfer to the slow cooker, along with the lentils, spices, and lemon juice. Add the broth and enough water to come about 7-cm above the vegetables. Cover and cook on high for 1 hour.
2. Turn the cooker to low and cook the soup for 5 to 6 hours. Season with salt and pepper, if desired. Add water to thin if the soup is too thick. Ladle into bowls and serve hot.

CHAPTER 9: STARTER

CREAMY BEEF AND CHEESE DIP

Prep time: 15 minutes | Cook time: 2 hours | Makes about 1½ L

INGREDIENTS:

* 450 g beef mince
* 1 onion, chopped
* 900 g nacho cheese dip
* 300 g cream of mushroom soup
* 400 g tinned diced tomatoes with green chillies

DIRECTIONS:

1. Brown beef and onion in a frying pan over medium heat, about 6 to 8 minutes. Drain meat mixture and place in a slow cooker.
2. Add all remaining ingredients into a slow cooker and combine.
3. Cover and cook on low for 2 hours, or until cheese is melted, stirring occasionally.
4. Serve over baked potatoes or with tortilla crisps, if desired.

BARBECUED SMOKIES

Prep time: 5 minutes | Cook time: 5 to 6 hours | Serves 8

INGREDIENTS:

* 450 g miniature smoked sausages
* 800 g barbecue sauce
* 300 ml water
* 45 ml Worcestershire sauce
* ½ tsp. pepper

DIRECTIONS:

1. In a slow cooker, combine all ingredients. Cover and cook on low for 5 to 6 hours or until heated through. Serve warm.

SIMPLE PIZZA BITES

Prep time: 10 minutes | Cook time: 1 hour | Serves 8

INGREDIENTS:

* 450 g beef mince
* 450 g bulk Italian sausage
* 450 g spreadable cheddar cheese
* 4 tsps. pizza seasoning
* ½ tsp. Worcestershire sauce

DIRECTIONS:

1. In a large non-stick frying pan, brown beef and sausage until crumbly. Drain and place in a slow cooker.
2. Add remaining ingredients to the slow cooker and stir to combine. Cover and cook on low for 1 hour. Serve warm.

BBQ PARTY STARTERS

Prep time: 15 minutes | Cook time: 2¼ to 3¼ hours | Serves 16

INGREDIENTS:

* 450 g beef mince
* 30 g finely chopped onion
* 450 g miniature hot dogs, drained
* 340 g jar apricot jam
* 235 ml barbecue sauce
* 565 g tinned pineapple chunks, drained

DIRECTIONS:

1. In a large bowl, combine beef and onion, mixing lightly but thoroughly. Shape into 2½-cm balls. In a large frying pan over medium heat, cook the meatballs in two batches until cooked through, turning occasionally.
2. Using a slotted spoon, transfer the meatballs to a slow cooker. Add the miniature hot dogs, apricot jam, and barbecue sauce, stirring well. Cover and cook on high for 2 to 3 hours or until heated through.
3. Stir in the pineapple chunks. Cook, covered, for 15 to 20 minutes longer or until heated through. Serve warm.

SWEET GLAZED MEATBALLS

Prep time: 10 minutes | Cook time: 4 to 5 hours | Makes about 10½ dozen

INGREDIENTS:

* 235 ml grape juice
* 375 g seedless strawberry jam
* 235 g ketchup
* 230 g tomato passata
* 1.8 kg frozen fully cooked Italian meatballs

DIRECTIONS:

1. In a small saucepan, combine the juice, jam, ketchup, and tomato sauce. Cook and stir over medium heat until jam is melted.
2. Place the meatballs in a slow cooker. Pour the sauce over the top and gently stir to coat. Cover and cook on low for 4 to 5 hours or until heated through. Serve warm.

LEMONY CHICKEN WINGS

Prep time: 15 minutes | Cook time: 6 to 8 hours | Makes about 4 dozen

INGREDIENTS:

* 2.3 kg chicken wings (about 25 wings)
* 350 g chilli sauce
* 60 ml lemon juice
* 60 ml black treacle
* 30 ml Worcestershire sauce
* 6 garlic cloves, minced
* 1 tbsp. chilli powder
* 1 tbsp. salsa
* 1 tsp. garlic salt
* 3 drops hot pepper sauce

DIRECTIONS:

1. Cut chicken wings into three sections, discarding wing tips. Place the wings in a slow cooker.
2. In a small bowl, combine the remaining ingredients. Pour over chicken and stir to coat. Cover and cook on low for 6 to 8 hours or until chicken is tender. Serve warm.

CHAPTER 10: DESSERT

FUDGY BROWNIES

Prep time: 10 minutes | Cook time: 3 to 4 hours | Serves 6

INGREDIENTS:

* 70 g plain flour
* ½ tsp. baking powder
* ⅛ tsp. salt
* 60 g unsweetened chocolate, chopped
* 75 g unsalted butter
* 115 g brown sugar
* 1 large egg plus 1 large yolk, room temperature
* ½ tsp. vanilla extract
* 45 g toasted and chopped walnuts (optional)

DIRECTIONS:

1. Fill a slow cooker with 2½-cm water (about 500 ml) and place aluminium foil rack in bottom. Grease a springform pan and line with greaseproof paper.
2. Whisk flour, baking powder, and salt together in a bowl. In a large bowl, microwave chocolate and butter at 50 percent power, stirring occasionally, until melted, 1 to 2 minutes; let cool slightly. Whisk sugar, egg and yolk, and vanilla into cooled chocolate mixture until well combined. Stir in flour mixture until just incorporated.
3. Scrape batter into prepared pan, smooth top, and sprinkle with walnuts, if using. Set pan on prepared rack, cover, and cook until toothpick inserted into centre comes out with few moist crumbs attached, 3 to 4 hours on high.
4. Let brownies cool completely in pan on the wire rack, 1 to 2 hours. Cut into wedges and serve.

FRUITY CAKE WITH WALNUTS

Prep time: 10 minutes | Cook time: 3 to 5 hours | Serves 10 to 12

INGREDIENTS:

* 1 or 2 tins apple, blueberry, or peach fruit filling
* 1 (517-g) package yellow cake mix
* 120 g butter, melted
* 45 g chopped walnuts
* Rapeseed oil spray

DIRECTIONS:

1. Spray the insert of the slow cooker with rapeseed oil spray.
2. Place pie filling in a slow cooker.
3. In a mixing bowl, combine dry cake mix and butter. Spoon over filling.
4. Drop walnuts over top.
5. Cover and cook on low for 3 to 5 hours, or until a toothpick inserted into the centre of topping comes out clean. Serve warm.

DRIED APRICOTS

Prep time: 5 minutes | Cook time: 3 to 4 hours | Serves 6

INGREDIENTS:

* 340 g dried apricots
* 1 strip lemon or orange zest

DIRECTIONS:

1. Put the apricots and citrus zest in the slow cooker and add water to cover. Cover and cook on low until plump and tender, 3 to 4 hours.
2. Turn off the cooker, remove the lid, and let the apricots cool. Serve.

CREAMY CHEESECAKE

Prep time: 10 minutes | Cook time: 1½ to 2½ hours | Serves 8

INGREDIENTS:

*   8 digestive biscuits
*   30 g unsalted butter, melted
*   150 g sugar, divided
*   ½ tsp. ground cinnamon
*   Salt, to taste
*   510 g cream cheese, softened
*   1 tsp. vanilla extract
*   60 g soured cream
*   2 large eggs

DIRECTIONS:

1. Pulse biscuits in a food processor to fine crumbs, about 20 pulses. Add melted butter, 15 g sugar, cinnamon, and pinch salt and pulse to combine, about 4 pulses. Sprinkle crumbs into a springform pan and press into an even layer using the bottom of a glass. Wipe out processor bowl.
2. Process cream cheese, vanilla, ¼ tsp. salt, and remaining sugar in the processor until combined, about 15 seconds, scraping down sides of bowl as needed. Add soured cream and eggs and process until just incorporated, about 15 seconds; do not over mix. Pour filling into prepared pan and smooth top.
3. Fill a slow cooker with 2½-cm water (about 500 ml) and place aluminium foil rack in bottom. Set pan on prepared rack, cover, and cook until cheesecake registers 65ºC, 1½ to 2½ hours on high. Turn off slow cooker and let cheesecake sit, covered, for 1 hour.
4. Transfer cheesecake to a wire rack. Run a small knife around edge of cake and gently blot away condensation using kitchen towels. Let cheesecake cool in pan to room temperature, about 1 hour. Cover with cling film and refrigerate until well chilled, at least for 3 hours or up to 3 days.
5. About 30 minutes before serving, run a small knife around edge of cheesecake, then remove sides of pan. Invert cheesecake onto sheet of greaseproof paper, then turn cheesecake right side up onto a serving dish. Serve.

FALLEN CHOCOLATE SOUFFLÉ CAKE

Prep time: 5 minutes | Cook time: 6 hours | Serves 10 to 12

INGREDIENTS:

*   1 (517-g) package chocolate cake mix
*   115 ml rapeseed oil
*   500 g soured cream
*   4 eggs, beaten
*   1 (75-g) box instant chocolate custard mix
*   160 g chocolate chips (optional)

DIRECTIONS:

1. Combine all ingredients in a greased slow cooker.
2. Cover and cook on low for 6 hours. (Do not lift the lid until the end of the cooking time!)
3. Insert a toothpick into the centre of cake to see if it comes out clean. If it does, the soufflé is finished. If it doesn't, continue cooking for another 15 minutes. Check again. Repeat until it's finished cooking.
4. Serve warm.

LEMON BLUEBERRY CORNMEAL CAKE

Prep time: 10 minutes | Cook time: 2 to 3 hours | Serves 6

INGREDIENTS:

* 135 g plain flour
* 45 g cornmeal
* ½ tsp. baking powder
* ½ tsp. bread soda
* Salt, to taste
* 125 g plain yoghurt
* 65 g caster sugar
* 1 large egg
* 2 tsps. grated lemon zest plus 4 tsps. juice
* ½ tsp. vanilla extract
* 60 g unsalted butter, melted
* 145 g blueberries
* 90 g icing sugar
* Cooking spray

DIRECTIONS:

1. Fill a slow cooker with 2½-cm water (about 500 ml) and place aluminium foil rack in bottom. Make foil sling for 22½ by 11½-cm loaf pan by folding 2 long sheets of foil; first sheet should be 22½-cm wide and second sheet should be 11½-cm wide. Lay sheets of foil in a pan perpendicular to each other, with extra foil hanging over edges of pan. Push foil into corners and up sides of pan, smoothing foil flush to pan. Lightly grease foil with cooking spray.
2. Whisk flour, cornmeal, baking powder, bread soda, and ½ tsp. of salt together in a bowl. In a large bowl, whisk yoghurt, caster sugar, egg, lemon zest, and vanilla until smooth, then slowly whisk in melted butter until well combined. Stir in flour mixture until just incorporated. Gently fold in blueberries.
3. Scrape batter into prepared pan and smooth top. Gently tap pan on the worktop to release air bubbles. Set pan on prepared rack, cover, and cook until toothpick inserted in centre comes out clean, 2 to 3 hours on high.
4. Let cake cool in pan on wire rack for 10 minutes. Using foil overhang, lift cake out of pan and transfer to rack, discarding foil. Let cake cool completely, 1 to 2 hours.
5. Whisk icing sugar, pinch salt, and lemon juice in a small bowl until smooth. Flip cake over onto a serving dish. Drizzle top and sides with glaze and let glaze set before serving, about 25 minutes.

PUMPKIN SPICE CHEESECAKE

Prep time: 10 minutes | Cook time: 1½ to 2½ hours | Serves 8

INGREDIENTS:

*   8 digestive biscuits
*   30 g unsalted butter, melted
*   150 g sugar, divided
*   ½ tsp. ground cinnamon
*   Salt, to taste
*   250 g tinned unsweetened pumpkin purée
*   340 g cream cheese, softened
*   ½ tsp. ground ginger
*   ⅛ tsp. ground cloves
*   60 g soured cream
*   2 large eggs

DIRECTIONS:

1. Pulse biscuits in a food processor to fine crumbs, about 20 pulses. Add melted butter, 15 g sugar, ½ tsp. cinnamon, and pinch salt and pulse to combine, about 4 pulses. Sprinkle crumbs into a springform pan and press into an even layer using the bottom of a glass. Wipe out processor bowl.
2. Spread pumpkin purée over baking sheet lined with several layers of kitchen towels and press dry with additional towels. Transfer purée to the processor bowl (purée will separate easily from towels). Add cream cheese, ginger, cloves, ½ tsp. salt, remaining sugar, and remaining 1 tsp. cinnamon and process until combined, about 15 seconds, scraping down sides of bowl as needed. Add soured cream and eggs and process until just incorporated, about 15 seconds; do not over mix. Pour filling into prepared pan and smooth top.
3. Fill a slow cooker with 2½-cm water (about 500 ml) and place aluminium foil rack in bottom. Set pan on prepared rack, cover, and cook until cheesecake registers 65ºC, 1½ to 2½ hours on high. Turn off slow cooker and let cheesecake sit, covered, for 1 hour.
4. Transfer cheesecake to a wire rack. Run a small knife around edge of cake and gently blot away condensation using kitchen towels. Let cheesecake cool in pan to room temperature, about 1 hour. Cover with cling film and refrigerate until well chilled, at least for 3 hours or up to 3 days.
5. About 30 minutes before serving, run a small knife around edge of cheesecake, then remove sides of pan. Invert cheesecake onto sheet of greaseproof paper, then turn cheesecake right side up onto a serving dish. Serve.

ULTIMATE CHOCOLATE CHEESECAKE

Prep time: 5 minutes | Cook time: 1½ to 2½ hours | Serves 8

INGREDIENTS:

* 8 chocolate sandwich biscuits
* 30 g unsalted butter, melted
* 115 g semisweet chocolate, chopped
* 510 g cream cheese, softened
* 135 g sugar
* ¼ tsp. salt
* 60 g soured cream
* 2 large eggs
* 15 g unsweetened cocoa powder
* 1 tsp. vanilla extract

DIRECTIONS:

1. Pulse biscuits in a food processor to fine crumbs, about 20 pulses. Add melted butter and pulse to combine, about 4 pulses. Sprinkle crumbs into a springform pan and press into an even layer using the bottom a glass. Wipe out processor bowl.
2. Microwave chocolate in a bowl at 50 percent power, stirring occasionally, until melted, 1 to 2 minutes. Let cool slightly. Process cream cheese, sugar, and salt in the processor until combined, about 15 seconds, scraping down sides of bowl as needed. Add cooled chocolate, soured cream, eggs, cocoa, and vanilla and process until just incorporated, about 15 seconds; do not over mix. Pour filling into prepared pan and smooth top.
3. Fill a slow cooker with 2½-cm water (about 500 ml) and place aluminium foil rack in bottom. Set pan on prepared rack, cover, and cook until cheesecake registers 65°C, 1½ to 2½ hours on high. Turn off slow cooker and let cheesecake sit, covered, for 1 hour.
4. Transfer cheesecake to a wire rack. Run a small knife around edge of cake and gently blot away condensation using kitchen towels. Let cheesecake cool in pan to room temperature, about 1 hour. Cover with cling film and refrigerate until well chilled, at least for 3 hours or up to 3 days.
5. About 30 minutes before serving, run a small knife around edge of cheesecake, then remove sides of pan. Invert cheesecake onto sheet of greaseproof paper, then turn cheesecake right side up onto a serving dish. Serve.

SPICED APPLESAUCE CAKE

Prep time: 10 minutes | Cook time: 3 to 4 hours | Serves 6

INGREDIENTS:

* 135 g plain flour
* ½ tsp. bread soda
* ¼ tsp. ground cinnamon
* ¼ tsp. salt
* Pinch ground nutmeg
* Pinch ground cloves
* 50 g caster sugar
* 125 g applesauce
* 1 large egg
* ½ tsp. vanilla extract
* 90 g unsalted butter, melted
* Confectioners' sugar, for dusting

DIRECTIONS:

1. Fill a slow cooker with 2½-cm water (about 500 ml) and place aluminium foil rack in bottom. Grease a cake tin and line with greaseproof paper.
2. Whisk flour, bread soda, cinnamon, salt, nutmeg, and cloves together in a bowl. In a large bowl, whisk caster sugar, applesauce, egg, and vanilla until smooth, then slowly whisk in melted butter until well combined. Stir in flour mixture until just incorporated.
3. Scrape batter into prepared pan and smooth top. Gently tap pan on the worktop to release air bubbles. Set pan on prepared rack, cover, and cook until toothpick inserted in centre comes out clean, 3 to 4 hours on high.
4. Let cake cool in pan on wire rack for 10 minutes. Run a small knife around edge of cake, then remove from the sides of pan. Remove cake from pan bottom, discarding greaseproof, and let cool completely on a rack, 1 to 2 hours. Transfer to a serving dish and dust with icing sugar. Serve.

CHAPTER 11: SAUCE AND DRESSING

GARLIC FRESH TOMATO SAUCE

Prep time: 10 minutes | Cook time: 5 hours | Makes about ¾ L

INGREDIENTS:

* 900 g ripe plum tomatoes, peeled cored, halved, and seeded
* 4 garlic cloves, smashed and peeled
* 60 ml extra-virgin olive oil
* 4 to 5 basil sprigs
* 1 tsp. coarse salt, plus more to taste
* ¼ tsp. freshly ground pepper
* Pinch sugar
* 120 ml boiling water

DIRECTIONS:

1. Add tomatoes, garlic, oil, basil, salt, pepper, and sugar to a slow cooker. Stir to combine. Add the boiling water. Cover and cook on high until sauce thickens slightly, 1 hour. Reduce heat to low and cook for 4 hours more.
2. For a thicker sauce, continue cooking on low for 2 hours, or until desired thickness is reached. Serve sauce immediately, or let cool to room temperature and refrigerate in an airtight container for up to 3 days.

VEGAN GARLIC PASTA SAUCE

Prep time: 20 minutes | Cook time: 4 hours | Makes 2 L

INGREDIENTS:

* 30 ml extra-virgin olive oil
* 2 cloves garlic, minced
* ½ tsp. red pepper flakes
* 1 large onion, coarsely chopped
* 2 portobello mushrooms, coarsely chopped
* 1 medium red bell pepper, deseeded and coarsely chopped
* 1 medium yellow bell pepper, deseeded and coarsely chopped
* 1 tbsp. dried oregano
* 2 tsps. dried basil
* Salt, to taste
* 30 ml balsamic vinegar
* 1.8 kg tinned crushed plum tomatoes
* Freshly ground black pepper, to taste

DIRECTIONS:

1. Heat the oil in a large sauté pan over medium-high heat. Add the garlic and red pepper flakes, and sauté until the garlic is fragrant, about 1 minute. Add the onion and sauté until the onion begins to soften, another 2 minutes. Add the remaining vegetables, the oregano, basil, and 2 tsps. of salt and sauté until the vegetables give off some liquid, about 5 minutes.
2. Using a slotted spoon, transfer the vegetables to a slow cooker. Stir in the vinegar and tomatoes. Cover and cook on high for 4 hours or on low for 8 hours. Season with salt and pepper.
3. Serve immediately or refrigerate until ready to serve.

SHALLOT AND RED WINE SAUCE

Prep time: 5 minutes | Cook time: 5 hours | Makes about 2½ L

INGREDIENTS:

* 120 g unsalted butter, melted
* 1 finely chopped shallot
* 2 tsps. dried thyme
* 475 ml full-bodied red wine
* 2 L beef broth
* ½ tsp. freshly ground black pepper
* 35 g plain flour

DIRECTIONS:

1. Combine 60 g of the butter, shallots, thyme, red wine, broth, and pepper in a slow cooker. Cook, uncovered, on high for 4 hours, until the mixture is reduced by one-third.
2. Stir the remaining melted butter and flour together, then whisk into the sauce. Cover and cook for an additional 45 minutes, until the sauce is thickened.
3. Serve immediately or refrigerate until ready to serve.

CLASSIC BOLOGNESE SAUCE

Prep time: 15 minutes | Cook time: 6 to 7 hours | Makes 2½ L

INGREDIENTS:

* 15 g unsalted butter
* 30 ml olive oil
* 1 large sweet onion, such as Vidalia, finely chopped
* 75 g finely diced carrot
* 75 g finely diced celery
* 1 clove garlic, minced
* 450 g lean pork mince
* 230 g ground veal
* 230 g lean beef mince
* ⅛ tsp. ground nutmeg
* ⅛ tsp. ground cinnamon
* 235 ml whole milk
* 235 ml dry white wine or vermouth
* 2.7 kg tinned crushed plum tomatoes
* Salt and freshly ground black pepper, to taste

DIRECTIONS:

1. Melt the butter in the oil in a large frying pan over medium heat. Add the onion, carrot, celery, and garlic and sauté until the vegetables are softened. Add the meats and sauté until no longer pink, breaking up any large chunks with a wooden spoon.
2. Spoon off any fat or water from the pan until the pan is dry. Add the nutmeg and cinnamon and sauté for another 2 minutes to allow the flavours to blend. Stir in the milk and boil until the milk has just about evaporated.
3. Transfer the contents of the frying pan to a slow cooker. Add the wine and tomatoes and stir to blend. Cover and cook the sauce on high for 6 to 7 hours. Season with salt and pepper.
4. Serve immediately or refrigerate until ready to serve.

BASIL TOMATO SAUCE

Prep time: 15 minutes | Cook time: 2½ to 3 hours | Makes about 1¼ L

INGREDIENTS:

* 30 g unsalted butter
* 30 ml olive oil
* 1 medium-size yellow onion, finely chopped
* 1 to 2 cloves garlic, minced
* 1.6 kg tinned whole plum tomatoes, drained (if packed in purée, don't drain) and coarsely chopped
* 30 ml dry red or white wine
* Pinch of sugar
* 15 g shredded fresh basil, divided
* Pinch of dried thyme or oregano
* Salt and freshly ground black pepper, to taste
* 2 tbsps. chopped fresh flat-leaf parsley

DIRECTIONS:

1. In a medium-size frying pan over medium heat, melt the butter in the olive oil. Cook the onion, stirring, until softened, about 5 minutes. Add the garlic and cook, stirring, for 2 minutes.
2. Transfer to the slow cooker. Add the tomatoes, wine, sugar, half of the basil, and thyme and stir to combine. Cover and simmer on high for 2 to 2½ hours.
3. Season the sauce with salt and pepper and stir in the remaining basil and the parsley. Cover and cook on low for 20 to 30 minutes longer. Serve the sauce hot. It will keep, refrigerated, for up to a week and frozen for 2 months.

SALSA MEXICANA

Prep time: 20 minutes | Cook time: 5 to 6 hours | Makes about ¾ L

INGREDIENTS:

* 45 ml olive oil
* 1 large yellow banana chili, peeled, deseeded, and chopped
* 2 small white onions, chopped
* 2 cloves garlic, chopped
* 800 g tomato passata
* 30 g tomato puree
* 350 ml chicken broth
* 2 tbsps. chopped fresh coriander
* 1 tbsp. chilli powder, or more to taste
* ½ tsp. ground cumin
* ½ tsp. dried Mexican oregano or marjoram
* Salt, to taste

DIRECTIONS:

1. In a medium-size frying pan over medium heat, heat the oil, then cook the chilli, onions, and garlic, stirring, until softened, about 5 minutes. Transfer to the slow cooker and add the tomato purée and paste, broth, coriander, chilli powder, cumin, and oregano. Stir to combine, then cover and simmer on low for 5 to 6 hours.
2. Use a handheld immersion blender to partially purée the sauce right in the slow cooker or transfer to a blender to purée. Season with salt. The sauce will keep, refrigerated, for 5 to 7 days and frozen for up to a month.

APPENDIX 1: MEASUREMENT CONVERSION CHART

WEIGHT EQUIVALENTS

METRIC	US STANDARD	US STANDARD (OUNCES)
15 g	1 tablespoon	1/2 ounce
30 g	1/8 cup	1 ounce
60 g	1/4 cup	2 ounces
115 g	1/2 cup	4 ounces
170 g	3/4 cup	6 ounces
225 g	1 cup	8 ounces
450 g	2 cups	16 ounces
900 g	4 cups	2 pounds

VOLUME EQUIVALENTS

METRIC	US STANDARD	US STANDARD (OUNCES)
15 ml	1 tablespoon	1/2 fl.oz.
30 ml	2 tablespoons	1 fl.oz.
60 ml	1/4 cup	2 fl.oz.
125 ml	1/2 cup	4 fl.oz.
180 ml	3/4 cup	6 fl.oz.
250 ml	1 cup	8 fl.oz.
500 ml	2 cups	16 fl.oz.
1000 ml	4 cups	1 quart

TEMPERATURES EQUIVALENTS

CELSIUS (C)	FAHRENHEIT (F) (APPROXIMATE)
120 °C	250 °F
135 °C	275 °F
150 °C	300 °F
160 °C	325 °F
175 °C	350 °F
190 °C	375 °F
205 °C	400 °F
220 °C	425 °F
230 °C	450 °F
245°C	475 °F
260 °C	500 °F

LENGTH EQUIVALENTS

METRIC	IMPERIAL
3 mm	1/8 inch
6 mm	1/4 inch
1 cm	1/2 inch
2.5 cm	1 inch
3 cm	1 1/4 inches
5 cm	2 inches
10 cm	4 inches
15 cm	6 inches
20 cm	8 inches

APPENDIX 2: RECIPES INDEX

REFERENCE

https://www.shutterstock.com/zh/image-photo/slow-cooker-chicken-taco-soup-topped-1900952128
https://www.shutterstock.com/zh/image-photo/chickpea-curry-stew-roasted-cherry-tomatoes-1694577256
https://www.shutterstock.com/zh/image-photo/slow-cooker-german-potato-soup-kartoffelsuppe-1198596244
https://www.shutterstock.com/zh/image-photo/rice-pudding-vegan-coconut-diet-breakfast-1417343015
https://www.shutterstock.com/zh/image-photo/homemade-roasted-granola-on-marble-background-1223749711
https://www.shutterstock.com/zh/image-photo/cheesy-grits-butter-white-bowl-breakfast-380432767
https://www.shutterstock.com/zh/image-photo/healthy-eating-breakfast-food-oatmeal-porridge-782826829
https://www.shutterstock.com/zh/image-photo/oatmeal-porridge-bowl-table-top-view-1613820475
https://www.shutterstock.com/zh/image-photo/homemade-sour-cream-glass-jars-on-1051189958
https://www.shutterstock.com/zh/image-photo/homemade-sea-bream-fish-congee-chinese-2067213161
https://www.shutterstock.com/zh/image-photo/homemade-slow-cooker-creamed-corn-bowl-2208501385
https://www.shutterstock.com/zh/image-photo/homemade-omlette-cheese-mushrooms-spinach-pan-1704629302
https://www.shutterstock.com/zh/image-photo/vegan-food-chickpeas-chard-potaje-typical-2104314353
https://www.shutterstock.com/zh/image-photo/vegetable-chili-bean-stew-red-kidney-1915966867
https://www.shutterstock.com/zh/image-photo/mashed-potatoes-butter-fresh-parsley-white-1606105234
https://www.shutterstock.com/zh/image-photo/homemade-creamy-scalloped-potatoes-cheese-spices-1993220726
https://www.shutterstock.com/zh/image-photo/green-asparagus-sesame-274943183
https://www.shutterstock.com/zh/image-photo/slow-cooker-mushroom-barley-soup-selective-710226799
https://www.shutterstock.com/zh/image-photo/portion-saffron-risotto-on-wooden-table-2031465449
https://www.shutterstock.com/zh/image-photo/salad-white-wild-rice-mushrooms-herbs-384359485
https://www.shutterstock.com/zh/image-photo/pearl-barley-cheese-herbs-white-ceramic-2160707877
https://www.shutterstock.com/zh/image-photo/mexican-black-bean-corn-quinoa-salad-1170210535
https://www.shutterstock.com/zh/image-photo/slow-cooker-white-chili-chicken-beans-730392892
https://www.shutterstock.com/zh/image-photo/smoked-turkey-leg-on-plate-vegetables-1931168147
https://www.shutterstock.com/zh/image-photo/mexican-enchilada-baking-dish-ingredients-on-251982688
https://www.shutterstock.com/zh/image-photo/tasty-chicken-pot-pie-green-peas-622736921
https://www.shutterstock.com/zh/image-photo/hot-homemade-white-bean-chicken-chili-371782837
https://www.shutterstock.com/zh/image-photo/homemade-slow-cooker-pot-roast-carrots-394256116
https://www.shutterstock.com/zh/image-photo/braised-lamb-eggplant-vegetables-red-pot-314191577
https://www.shutterstock.com/zh/image-photo/beef-stroganoff-mushroom-sauce-dish-made-2183632303
https://www.shutterstock.com/zh/image-photo/traditional-asian-beef-teriyaki-green-onions-1214299597
https://www.shutterstock.com/zh/image-photo/pork-ribs-barbecue-served-classic-bbq-1960708252
https://www.shutterstock.com/zh/image-photo/slow-cooker-salmon-risotto-rustic-focus-500418307
https://www.shutterstock.com/zh/image-photo/cooked-salmon-fillets-dill-sauce-on-17939416
https://www.shutterstock.com/zh/image-photo/potatoes-stuffed-cheese-tuna-made-microwave-1861849363
https://www.shutterstock.com/zh/image-photo/thai-yellow-curry-seafood-white-rice-405422923
https://www.shutterstock.com/zh/image-photo/traditional-mexican-food-shrimp-tacos-melted-2036237492
https://www.shutterstock.com/zh/image-photo/crock-pot-split-pea-soup-smoked-1856409994
https://www.shutterstock.com/zh/image-photo/fresh-cream-zucchini-soup-croutons-wooden-547202809
https://www.shutterstock.com/zh/image-photo/french-onion-soup-gratined-cheese-winter-1217445211
https://www.shutterstock.com/zh/image-photo/creamy-artichoke-puree-soup-served-toasted-2240713105
https://www.shutterstock.com/zh/image-photo/beef-tomato-macaroni-soup-white-bowl-2122290686
https://www.shutterstock.com/zh/image-photo/slow-cooker-shredded-chicken-texmex-focus-548876014
https://www.shutterstock.com/zh/image-photo/top-view-portion-hot-spicy-peanuts-369285530
https://www.shutterstock.com/zh/image-photo/meatballs-cranberry-sauce-white-bowl-on-1537136063
https://www.shutterstock.com/zh/image-photo/barbecue-chicken-wings-slow-cooker-sweet-1645925887
https://www.shutterstock.com/zh/image-photo/mini-sausages-barbecue-sauce-bowl-on-1567219474
https://www.shutterstock.com/zh/image-photo/apple-sponge-cake-cooked-multicooker-dusted-222138817
https://www.shutterstock.com/zh/image-photo/slow-cooker-chocolate-fondue-fruit-waffles-2239751897
https://www.shutterstock.com/zh/image-photo/rhubarb-strawberry-compote-fresh-strawberries-171828257
https://www.shutterstock.com/zh/image-photo/carrot-cake-cream-cheese-frosting-easter-1682647465
https://www.shutterstock.com/zh/image-photo/stack-fudgy-brownies-on-sheet-parchment-2173426697
https://www.shutterstock.com/zh/image-photo/healthy-sugar-free-applesauce-glass-jar-1036943542
https://www.shutterstock.com/zh/image-photo/tomato-barbecue-sauce-ceramic-bowl-141609043
https://www.shutterstock.com/zh/image-photo/traditional-italian-marinara-sauce-jar-on-1991905916
https://www.shutterstock.com/zh/image-photo/mixberries-sauce-jar-1116522641
https://www.shutterstock.com/zh/image-photo/homemade-bolognese-sauce-made-fresh-tomato-579932632